KEITH DOUGLAS

Alamein to Zem Zem

With illustrations by the Author

D0869117

ff

faber and faber

This edition first published in 2008
by Faber and Faber Ltd
Bloomsbury House, 74–77 Great Russell Street
London WC1B 3DA

A CIP record for this book is available from the British Library

ISBN 978-0-571-24194-1

ALAMEIN

I AM not writing about these battles as a soldier, nor trying to discuss them as military operations. I am thinking of them – selfishly, but as I always shall think of them – as my first experience of fighting: that is how I shall write of them. To say I thought of the battle of Alamein as an ordeal sounds pompous: but I did think of it as an important test, which I was interested in passing. I observed these battles partly as an exhibition – that is to say that I went through them a little like a visitor from the country going to a great show, or like a child in a factory – a child sees the brightness and efficiency of steel machines and endless belts slapping round and round, without caring or knowing what it is all there for. When I could order my thoughts I looked for more significant things than appearances; I still looked – I cannot avoid it – for something decorative, poetic or dramatic.

The geography of the country in which I spent those few months is already as vague to me as if I had learnt it from an atlas much longer ago. The dates have slipped away, the tactical lessons have been learnt by someone else. But what remains in my mind – a flurry of violent impressions – is vivid enough. Against a backcloth of indeterminate landscapes of moods and smells, dance the black and bright incidents.

I had to wait until 1942 to go into action. I enlisted in September 1939, and during two years or so of hanging about I never lost the certainty that the experience of battle was something I must have. Whatever changes in the nature of warfare, the battlefield is the simple, central stage of the war: it is there that the interesting things happen. We talk in the evening, after fighting, about the great and rich men who cause and conduct wars. They have so many reasons of their own that they can afford to lend us some of them. There is nothing odd about their attitude. They are out for something they want, or their Governments want, and they are using us to get it for them. Anyone can understand that: there is nothing unusual or humanly exciting at that end of the war. I mean there may be things to excite financiers and parliamentarians – but not to excite a poet or a painter or a doctor.

But it is exciting and amazing to see thousands of men, very few of whom have much idea why they are fighting, all enduring hardships, living in an unnatural, dangerous, but not wholly terrible world, having to kill and to be killed, and yet at intervals moved by a feeling of comradeship with the men who kill them and whom they kill, because they are enduring and experiencing the same things. It is tremendously illogical – to read about it cannot convey the impression of having walked through the looking-glass which touches a man entering a battle.

I had arrived in the Middle East in August 1941. As a result of passing a course on which I was sent by accident, I found myself posted away from my regiment to a Divisional staff. I still wanted to get into action, and probably looked impatiently at my colleagues and superiors on this staff. For eight months I honestly tried hard to make sense of the job I was given – in other words to persuade the staff colonel and major to whose department I was attached to give me some work to do. The situation emerged clearly and simply as the months passed. My job was to give camouflage training. The staff officers of 'G' staff, under the General, arranged training programmes: they invariably forgot to include camouflage. At first they airily agreed to my humble reminders with a wealth of condescending language – the General alone refrained from calling me 'old boy' although he said good morning, good morning as civilly as Siegfried Sassoon's General.

After eight months of relative inaction, not being at any time a patient person, and having a hatred for wasted time, I tried to get back to my regiment. I could not be released: with the charm and politeness with which everyone on a staff always speaks to everyone else, I was told I was indispensable. Any disclaimer of this, any statement that I was doing nothing but waste Government petrol and money, appeared to strike them as a conventionally modest reply, equivalent to saying 'I'm only doing my job, old boy'. The offensive loomed very large in rumour, among so many officers living more or less inside the horse's mouth. I decided, if there were no other means of going into action with my regiment, to run away from Divisional Headquarters in my truck, and report to my colonel. I thought vaguely that this might be straightened out later. To plan this was the natural result of having the sort of little-boy mentality I still have. A little earlier, I might have wanted to run away and be a pirate. But it was surprising how easily the plan was realized and justified. For eight months I had done no mechanized training, my regiment was equipped with tanks, guns and wireless sets which I had never handled, scarcely seen, in my life; and it seemed possible, and even likely, that my colonel who had applied for me before the battle, would not want an untrained officer to join him during action and endanger everyone's life while learning his job. If he refused me I was determined not to come back to Division but to drive away down the coast road to Alexandria, and from there through Cairo and Ismalia and across the Sinai desert to Palestine, to amuse myself until I was caught and court-martialled.

The battle of Alamein began on 23 October 1942. Six days afterwards I set out in direct disobedience of orders to rejoin my regiment. My batman was delighted with this manoeuvre. 'I like you, sir,' he said. 'You're shit or bust, you are.' This praise gratified me a lot.

I

Six days after I had heard rumbling on the western skyline, that famous barrage that began it, I moved up from the rear to the front of the British attack. Through areas as full of organization as a city of ants – it happened that two days before I had been reading Maeterlinck's descriptions of ant communities – I drove up the sign-posted tracks until, when I reached my own place in all this activity, I had seen the whole arrangement of the Army, almost too large to appreciate, as a body would look to a germ

7

riding in its bloodstream. First the various headquarters of the higher formations, huge conglomerations of large and small vehicles facing in all directions, flags, signposts and numbers standing among their dust. On the main tracks, marked with crude replicas of a hat, a bottle, and a boat, cut out of petrol tins, lorries appeared like ships, plunging their bows into drifts of dust and rearing up suddenly over crests like waves. Their wheels were continually hidden in dustclouds: the ordinary sand being pulverized by so much traffic into a substance almost liquid, sticky to the touch, into which the feet of men walking sank to the knee. Every man had a white mask of dust in which, if he wore no goggles, his eyes showed like a clown's eyes. Some did wear goggles, many more the celluloid eyeshields from their anti-gas equipments. Trucks and their loads became a uniform dust colour before they had travelled twenty yards: even with a handkerchief tied like a cowboy's over nose and mouth, it was difficult to breathe.

The lorry I drove was a Ford two-tonner, a commercial lorry designed for roadwork, with an accelerator and springs far too sensitive for tracks like these. I was thrown, with my two passengers, helplessly against the sides and roof of the cab: the same was happening to our clothes and possessions in the back. The sun was climbing behind us. As far as we could see across the dunes to right and left stretched formations of vehicles and weapons of all kinds, three-ton and heavier supply lorries of the R.A.S.C., Field workshops with huge recovery vehicles and winches, twenty-five-pounders and quads, Bofors guns in pits with their crews lying beside them, petrol fires everywhere, on which the crews of all were brewing up tea and tinned meat in petrol tins.

We looked very carefully at all these, not having any clear idea where we should find the regiment. We did not yet know whether they were resting or actually in action. I realized that in spite of having been in the R.A.C. for two years, I had very little idea what to expect. I like to picture coming events to myself, perhaps through having been much alone, and to rehearse them mentally. I could not remember any picture or account which gave me a clear idea of tanks in action. In training we had been employed in executing drill movements in obedience to flag signals from troop leaders. We had been trained to fire guns on the move, and to adopt a vastly extended and exactly circular formation at night. But most of my training had been by lectures without illustrations: what few words of reminiscence I had heard from those who returned from actions in France and the desert, suggested that no notice was ever taken of the manoeuvres we had been taught in the field – which left me none the wiser. None of us had ever thought much of the drill movements and flag-signals. News films – just as later on that mediocre film 'Desert Victory' – gave no idea where most of their 'action' pictures were taken. Even my own regiment had been known to put their tanks through various evolutions for cameramen.

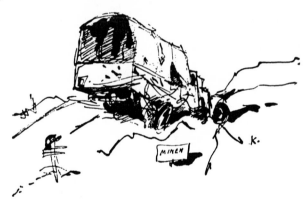

So feeling a little like the simple soul issuing from the hand of God, *animula blandula vagula*, I gazed on all the wonders of this landscape, looking among all the signs for the stencilled animal and number denoting my own regiment. I was not sure yet whether this was an abortive expedition – tomorrow might find me, with a movement order forged on my own typewriter, scorching down the road to Palestine. All my arrangements had been made to suit the two contingencies. I had dressed in a clean khaki shirt and shorts, pressed and starched a week or two before in an

Alexandria laundry. My batman Lockett, an ex-hunt servant with a horseman's interest in turn-out and good leather, had polished the chin-strap and the brasses of my cap and belt till the brasses shone like suns and the chinstrap like a piece of glass laid on velvet. In the lorry, besides Lockett, rode a fitter from Divisional Headquarters, who was to drive it back there if Lockett and I stayed with the regiment.

The guns, such desultory firing as there was, sounded more clearly: the different noise of bombs was distinguishable now. The formations on either side were of a more combatant kind, infantry resting, heavy artillery and the usual light anti-aircraft. A few staff and liaison officers in jeeps and staff cars still passed, the jeeps often identifiable only by their passengers' heads showing out of enveloping dustclouds: but the traffic was now mostly supply vehicles moving between the combatant units and their 'B' or supply echelons.

Fifteen miles from our starting point and about four miles in rear of the regiment, I found our 'B' echelon, in charge of two officers whom I had known fairly well during my few months with the regiment, Mac – an ex-N.C.O. of the Scots Greys, now a captain; and Owen, a major; an efficient person with deceptive, adolescent manners, whom no one would suspect of being an old Etonian. It is difficult to imagine Owen at any public school at all: if you look at him he seems to have sprung, miraculously enlarged, but otherwise unaltered, from an inky bench in a private preparatory school. He looks as if he had white rats in his pockets. On these two I had to test my story.

I was afraid the idea of my running back to the regiment would seem absurd to them, so I began non-committally by greeting them and asking where the regiment was. 'A few miles up the road,' said Mac. 'They're out of action at the moment but they're expecting to go in again any time. Have you come back to us?' I said that depended on the Colonel. 'Oh, he'll be glad to see you,' said Mac. 'I don't think "A" Squadron's got many officers left: they had a bad day the other day; I lost all my vehicles in BI the same night – petrol lorry got hit and lit up the whole scene and they just plastered us with everything they had.' In spite of this ominous news, I was encouraged by Mac's saying I was needed, and pushed on up the track until we came to the regiment.

Tanks and trucks were jumbled close together, with most of the men busy doing maintenance on them. A tall Ordnance officer whom I had never seen directed me to the same fifteen-hundredweight truck which had been the Orderly Room in the Training Area at Wadi Natrun. I left my lorry and walked, feeling more and more apprehensive as I approached this final interview. I looked about among the men as I went, but saw only one or two familiar faces; a regiment's personnel alters surprisingly, even in eight months.

I looked about for Edward, my squadron leader, and for Tom and Raoul, who had been troop leaders with me, but could not see them. The Colonel, beautifully dressed and with his habitual indolence of hand, returned my salute from inside the fifteen-hundredweight, where he was sitting with Graham, the adjutant, a handsome, red-haired, amiable young Etonian. I said to Piccadilly Jim (the Colonel), 'Good evening, sir, I've escaped from Division for the moment, so I wondered if I'd be any use to you up here.' 'Well, Peter,' stroking his moustache and looking like a contented ginger cat, 'we're *most* glad to see you – er – as always. All the officers in "A" Squadron, except Andrew, are casualties, so I'm sure he'll welcome you with open arms. We're probably going in early tomorrow morning, so you'd better go and get him to fix you up with a troop now.' After a few more politenesses, I went to find Andrew, and my kit. The tremendous question was decided, and in a disconcertingly abrupt and definite way, after eight months of abortive efforts to rejoin. Palestine was a long way off and a few miles to the west, where the sounds of gunfire had intensified, lay the German armies.

2

I found Andrew, sitting on a petrol tin beside his tanks: I had met him before but when he looked up at my approach he did not recognize me. He was not young, and although at the moment an acting major about to go into action in a tank for the first time in his life, Andrew had already seen service in Abyssinia in command of the native mercenaries who had been persuaded to fight for Haile Selassie. From Abyssinia he had come to Cairo and fallen, through that British military process which penalizes anyone who changes his job, from colonel to major. Later, he had gravitated to base depot, and being unemployed, returned to his war-substantive rank of captain. As a captain he had come back to the regiment; it is not difficult to picture the state of mind of a man who knows he has worked well and receives no reward except to be demoted two grades. He now found himself second in command of a squadron whose squadron leader had been a subaltern under him before. What happened after that was probably inevitable. Andrew's health and temper were none the better for the evil climate and conditions of his late campaign. Someone who knew him before – which I did not – said that he went away a charming and entertaining young man, and returned a hardened and embittered soldier.

He was a small man with blond hair turning grey, sitting on a petrol tin and marking the cellophane of his map case with a chinagraph pencil. His face was brick-red with sun and wind, the skin cracking on his lips and nose. He wore a grey Indian Army flannel shirt, a pair of old corduroy trousers, and sandals. Round his mahogany-coloured neck a blue silk handkerchief was twisted and tied like a stock, and on his head was a beret. Like most ex-cavalrymen he had no idea how to wear it. To him I reported, resplendent – if a little dusty – in polished cap and belt.

He allotted me two tanks, as a troop, there not being enough on the squadron strength to make sub-units of more than two tanks. I drove my lorry with the kit on it to one of the tanks and began to unload and sort out my belongings. Lockett and I laid them out, together with the three bags of emergency rations belonging to the lorry. The Corporal, lately commander of this tank, departed, staggering under his own possessions barely confined by his groundsheet in an amorphous bundle.

Lockett was to go for the duration of the battle to the technical stores lorry where he had a friend and where he could make himself useful. To him I handed over the greater part of my belongings – the style in which I had travelled at Divisional Headquarters being now outmoded. I kept a half-share of the three bags of rations, which I distributed between my two tanks (this amounting to several tins of bully beef, of course, one or two of First American white potatoes, and some greater treasures, tins of American bacon rashers, and of fruit and condensed milk. A pair of clean socks were filled, one with tea, the other with sugar). I changed my peaked cap for a beret, and retained a small cricket bag with shirts, slacks, washing and shaving kit, writing paper, a camera and a Penguin Shakespeare's Sonnets. Rolled up in my valise and bedding were a suit of battledress, my revolver, and a British warm. In my pocket I had a small flask of whisky, and in the locker on the side of the tank, in addition to the rations, I put some tins of N.A.A.F.I. coffee and Oxo cubes, bought in Alexandria. I now felt the satisfaction of any-one beginning an expedition – or as Barbet Hasard might have said on this occasion, a Voyage – in contemplating my assembled stores, and in bestowing them. As soon as this was finished I began to make the acquaintance of my tank crews.

My own tank was a Mk III Crusader – then comparatively new to us all. I had once been inside the Mk II, which had a two-pounder gun and a four-man crew, and was now superseded by this tank with a six-pounder gun and only three men in the crew, the place of the fourth being occupied by the breech mechanism of the six-pounder. This tank is the best looking medium tank I ever saw, whatever its shortcomings of per-formance. It is low-built, which in desert warfare, and indeed all tank warfare, is a first consideration. This gives it, together with its lines and its suspension on five great wheels a side, the appearance almost of a speedboat. To see these tanks crossing country at speed was a thrill which seemed inexhaustible – many times it encouraged us, and we were very proud of our Crusaders; though we often had cause to curse them.

From underneath this particular tank a pair of boots

protruded. As I looked at them, my mind being still by a matter of two days untrained to it, the inevitable association of ideas did not take place. The whole man emerged, muttering in a Glaswegian monotone. He was a small man with a seemingly disgruntled youngster's face, called Mudie. I found him, during the weeks I spent with him, to be lazy, permanently discontented, and a most amusing talker. In battle he did not have much opportunity for talking and was silent even during rests and meals; but at all other times he would wake up talking, as birds do, at the first gleam of light and long before dawn, and he would still be talking in the invariable monotone long after dark. He was the driver of the tank.

The gunner was another reservist. His name was Evan, and he looked a very much harder case than Mudie, though I think there was not much to choose between them. Evan scarcely spoke at all, and if drawn into conversation would usually reveal (if he were talking to an officer) a number of injustices under which he was suffering at the moment, introducing them with a calculated air of weariness and 'it doesn't matter now', as though he had been so worn down by the callousness of his superiors as to entertain little hope of redress. In conversation with his fellows (I say fellows because he had no friends), he affected a peculiar kind of snarling wit, and he never did anything that was not directly for his own profit. Mudie would often do favours for other people. Evan would prefer an officer and then only if he could not well avoid it. Yet he was unexpectedly quick and efficient on two occasions which I shall describe.

We were at an hour's notice to move. This meant, not that we should move in an hour's time, but that, if we did move, we should have an hour in which to prepare for it. When I had sorted out my belongings, and eaten some meat and vegetable stew and tinned fruit, washed down with coffee, I lay down on my bedding with a magazine which someone had left on the tank, and glancing only vaguely at the pages, thought over the changes of the last few days, and confronted myself with the future. Desultory thumps sounded in the distance, occasionally large bushes of dust sprang up on the skyline, or a plane droned across, very high up in the blue air. Men passed and repassed, shouted to each other, laughed, sang, and whistled dance tunes, as they always did. Metallic clangs and the hum of light and heavy engines at various pitches sounded at a distance. Occasionally a machine-gun would sputter for a few seconds, as it was tested or cleared. The whole conglomeration of sounds, mixing in the heat of declining afternoon, would have put me to sleep, but for my own excitement and apprehensions, and the indefatigable flies.

But though I reflected, a little uncomfortably, on what might be happening to me in a few hours, I was not dissatisfied. I still felt the exhilaration of cutting myself free from the whole net of inefficiency and departmental bullshit that had seemed to have me quite caught up in Divisional Headquarters. I had exchanged a vague and general existence for a simple and particular (and perhaps short) one. Best of all, I had never realized how ashamed of myself I had been in my safe job at Division until with my departure this feeling was suddenly gone. I had that feeling of almost unstable lightness which is felt physically immediately after putting down a heavy weight. All my difficult mental enquiries and arguments about the future were shelved, perhaps permanently. I got out my writing paper and wrote two letters, one to my mother and one to David Hicks in Cairo. Although in writing these letters (which, of course, got lost and were never posted) I felt very dramatic, the tone of them was not particularly theatrical. To my mother I wrote that I rejoiced to have escaped at last from Division and to be back with the regiment. I might not have time to write for a week or two, I added. To Hicks I sent a poem which I had written during my last two days at Division on an idea which I had had since a month before the offensive. I asked him to see that it got home as I had not got a stamp or an airgraph. He could print it in his magazine on the way, if he liked.

I had asked Andrew one or two questions in the hope of not showing myself too ignorant in my first action. But it was fairly plain that he knew nothing himself. 'I shouldn't worry, old boy,' was all he would say. 'The squadron and troop leaders don't use maps much, and there are no codes at all, just talk as you like over the air – except for giving map-references of course – but you won't need them. You'll find it's quite simple.' When I had written my letters I got into the turret with Evan and tried to learn its geography. My place as tank commander was on the right of the six-pounder. I had a seat, from which I could look out through a periscope. This afforded a very small view, and in action all tank commanders stand on the floor of their turrets so that their eyes are clear of the top, or actually sit in the manhole on top of their turret with their legs dangling inside. Behind the breech of the six-pounder is a metal shield to protect the crew against the recoil of the gun, which leaps back about a foot when it is fired. On my side of the six-pounder was a rack for a box of machine-gun ammunition, the belt of which had to run over the six-pounder and into the machine-gun mounted the other side of it. There were also two smoke dischargers to be operated by me. Stacked round the sides of the turret were the six-pounder shells, nose downwards; hand-grenades, smoke grenades and machine-gun ammunition. At the back of the turret on a shelf stood the wireless set, with its control box for switching from the A set to internal communication between the tank crew, and on top of the wireless set a pair of binoculars, wireless spare parts and tommy-gun magazines. There was a tommy-gun in a clip on Evan's side of the turret. On the shelf, when we were in action, we usually kept also some Penguin books, chocolate or boiled sweets if we could get them, a tin of processed cheese, a knife, and some biscuits. We were lucky enough to begin the battle with a tin of Australian butter as well. About dusk the wireless sets in all tanks were switched on and netted into the regimental control station, to make sure everyone's set was as far as possible on the same frequency. Each station, like 2LO in early broadcasting, was known by a call sign, by which it announced itself and was called up by control stations. Before dark I went over to make sure that my other tank was ready to move, completely filled with rations, kit, petrol, oil, ammunition, and water. I stayed some time talking to the crew. The Corporal, Browning, had already been captured and recaptured during the first four days of the battle. He said the Germans had treated him very well, and seemed quite cheerful – so did his gunner and driver – at the prospect of going into action again. This was more than could be said of Evan and Mudie who grew dourer and more taciturn every minute.

I lay down to sleep in my clothes, covered with my British warm and blankets, for the nights were already beginning to be cold. Perhaps betrayed by the spectacle of the stars as clear as jewels on black velvet into a mood of more solemnity, I suddenly found myself assuming that I was going to die tomorrow. For perhaps a quarter of an hour I considered to what possibilities of suffering, more than of death, I had laid myself open. This with the dramatic and emotional part of me: but my senses of proportion and humour, like two court jesters, chased away the tragic poet, and I drifted away on a tide of odd thoughts, watching the various signs of battle in the lower sky. I persuaded myself that I had passed the worst ordeals of fear and that there would be no time for sharp, instantaneous fear in battle. If I thought so, I was not long to be so deceived. The moon, now grown much greater than when a week or two ago she had inspired me to write a poem on her ominous pregnancy, presided over a variety of lesser lights; starshells, tracers of orange, green, red, blue, and a harsh white, and the deeper colours of explosions. We were still at an hour's notice.

3

Someone shook me out of my sleep at four o'clock in the cold morning. Somewhat to my surprise I woke immediately with the full consciousness of where I was: for I had feared as I dropped asleep the morning might surprise me unpleasantly at my least heroic hour. The moment I was wakeful I had to be busy. We were to move at five: before that engines and sets had to be warmed up, orders to be given through the whole hierarchy from the Colonel to the tank crews. In the half light the tanks seemed to crouch, still, but alive, like toads. I touched the cold metal shell of my own tank, my fingers amazed for a moment at its hardness, and swung myself into the turret to get out my map case. Of course, it had fallen down on the small circular steel floor of the turret. In getting down after it I contrived to hit my head on the base of the six-pounder and scratch open both my hands; inside the turret there is less room even than in an aircraft, and it requires experience to move about. By the time I came up a general activity had begun to warm the appearance of the place, if not the air of it. The tanks were now half-hidden in clouds of blue smoke as their engines began one after another to grumble, and the stagnant oil burnt away. This scene with the silhouettes of men and turrets interrupted by swirls of smoke and the sky lightening behind them, was to be made familiar to me by many repetitions. Out of each turret, like the voices of dwarfs, thin and cracked and bodiless, the voices of the operators and of the control set come; they speak to the usual accompaniment of 'mush', morse, odd squeals, and the peculiar jangling, like a barrel-organ, of an enemy jamming station.

Probably as a result of some vacillation by higher authority, nobody moved before seven o'clock, when the Crusader squadron – my squadron – moved out and on to the other side of a main track running north to south. Here we halted, having left the heavy squadrons of Shermans and Grants still in our rest area, and were allowed to brew up. The immense moral satisfaction and recreation of brewing up was one I had never realized. As soon as the permission is given, all crews except those of tanks detailed for look-out duties swarm out of their turrets. The long boxes on the side of the tank are opened: tins of bacon or M. & V., according to the time of day, are got out, while someone is lighting a fire in a tin filled with a paste of sand and petrol. A veteran, blackened half of a petrol-tin, with a twisted wire handle, is unhooked from some extremity of the tank and filled with water for tea. Within five minutes a good crew has a cup of immensely strong and sweet hot tea and sandwiches (for example) of oatmeal biscuits fried in bacon fat and enclosing crisp bacon. If there is a little more time, it will probably be used to make another brew of tea from the same leaves, and to eat more biscuits spread with oleomargarine – to me, a horrible but

wholesome synthetic – and Palestinian marmalade. This morning
I found printed on my tin of marmalade the name of the com-
munal settlement at Givat Brenner, where I had spent a day four
or five months before. Thoughts of those quiet trees and that
peaceful, industrious community induced a minute or two of
nostalgia, and a less logical but more comfortable sense of friends
following me. Soon after breakfast we were turned round and
returned to camp – I never discovered why we made this ex-
cursion. We did not move again until late afternoon, when
the regiment moved out, Crusaders leading, in single file on to
the track up which I had come the day before. The head of the
column turned westwards, only turrets and pennants, flown on
the small aerials, showing above the billowing dust. I took a
photograph of the column behind and in front of me.

That afternoon was still and sunny, the upper air clear, the
ground churned everywhere into white dust by the endless
traffic. This white dust lay very thickly rutted on the ground
and mixed with the atmosphere, like a mist for a foot or two
above the desert. Even without looking at the formations lying
beside the track and stretching away from it, it was impossible
not to feel immense subdued activity all over the area. On the
track, besides our own column of tanks moving up slowly,
screened and enveloped in their own dust, tanks and armoured
cars passed us going out of battle, and a renewed traffic of staff
cars and jeeps made it clear that the front line had advanced
since the previous night when few of them were coming so far
forward. These smaller vehicles bucketed in and out among the
main streams of traffic.

Up above in the clear sky a solitary aeroplane moved, bright
silver in the sunlight, a pale line of exhaust marking its unhurried course. The Bofors gunners on either side of us were running to their guns and soon opened a rapid, thumping fire, like a
titanic workman hammering. The silver body of the aeroplane
was surrounded by hundreds of little grey smudges, through
which it sailed on serenely. From it there fell away, slowly and
gracefully, an isolated shower of rain, a succession of glittering
drops. I watched them descend a hundred feet before it occurred

to me to consider their significance and forget their beauty. The column of tanks trundled forward imperturbably, but the heads of their crews no longer showed. I dropped down in the turret and shouted to Evan who was dozing in the gunner's seat: 'Someone's dropping some stuff.' He shouted back a question and adjusted his earphones. 'Bombs!' I said into the microphone. Their noisy arrival somewhere on our right confirmed the word. Control called us over the air: 'Nuts one, is everybody O.K.?' 'Two O.K. off.' 'Three O.K. off.' 'Four O.K. off,' said the troop leaders in turn. 'Five O.K. off.' I completed the group. The journey continued.

The view from a moving tank is like that in a camera obscura or a silent film – in that since the engine drowns all other noises except explosions, the whole world moves silently. Men shout, vehicles move, aeroplanes fly over, and all soundlessly: the noise of the tank being continuous, perhaps for hours on end, the effect is of silence. It is the same in an aircraft, but unless you are flying low, distance does away with the effect of a soundless pageant. I think it may have been the fact that for so much of the time I saw it without hearing it, which led me to feel that country into which we were now moving as an illimitably strange land, quite unrelated to real life, like the scenes in 'The Cabinet of Doctor Caligari'. Silence is a strange thing to us who live: we desire it, we fear it, we worship it, we hate it. There is a divinity about cats, as long as they are silent: the silence of swans gives them an air of legend. The most impressive thing about the dead is their triumphant silence, proof against anything in the world.

A party of prisoners now appeared marching on our left. They were evidently very tired but looked about them with a good deal of interest, particularly at our column. I thought of innumerable pictures of glowering S.S. men in Nazi tanks, and glared at them through my goggles in the hope of looking like part of an inexorable war machine myself. They must have been fairly impressed with the strength and concentration of our forces by the time they reached their cage at the rear. About two hundred of them passed us, in batches, as we continued our journey. We looked at them with an interest equal to their own.

They did not look very fearsome: they were almost all Germans with shapeless green or khaki drill uniforms and floppy peaked caps with a red, white and black bull's-eye on them. The desert on either side of the track became more sparsely populated with vehicles, and at length there were none but derelicts. The column halted at last, so that my tank stood beside the burnt-out shell of a German Mk IV Special, with its long gun and rows of little wheels. Most of one side of it had been torn out, probably by the explosion of its own ammunition. Some charred clothing lay beside it, but no equipment, and there was no sign of the crew. The whole thing made a disconcerting cautionary picture.

On the horizon to our front we could see two vehicles burning fiercely, from which expanding columns of black smoke slanted across the orange sky. We could see shells, visible by their traces as yellow or white lights, sailing in apparently slow curves across our front: they were being fired by tanks on our left, but were landing in dead ground to us. By now the light was ebbing perceptibly and soon the burning derelicts and the shell-traces gleamed against the sky. The traces of enemy shells could be seen flying from beyond the ridge ahead of us. We were now spectators of the closing stages of the day's battle.

4

I dismounted and went to find Andrew, leaving Evan and Mudie silently examining the nearest derelict: apparently we were to leaguer for the night nearby, and Andrew went away into the growing obscurity to receive his orders from the Colonel. He told me to prevent the squadron moving away and getting lost before he came back. Eventually, however, he sent the Welsh sergeant, Thomas, to summon us back to him, and himself led us slowly, watching one another's red rear lights, into our position for the night.

The Crusaders were drawn up in two rows in front of the heavy tanks, and we were ordered to put out a guard, until a guard from our attached infantry came to relieve us, and to dig one slit trench per tank. I would have been quite content with the protection of my tank turret but passed on the orders, sending Evan over to help Sergeant Thomas with the slit trench for the guard. We began to try and make some impression on the stony ground. The burning derelicts were no longer visible, and for the moment there was a background of silence to our efforts.

After we had been digging about a minute, a projectile of some sort screamed over our heads and burst with an orange flame and a great deal of noise somewhere in the darkness behind us, apparently among the heavy tanks. Another followed it, and I decided it would be ridiculous to attempt digging a trench under H.E. fire, when the tank turret was already available for our protection. Evan came back from Sergeant Thomas's tank and scrambled into the turret. I told Mudie to get in, and as soon as they had made room, stepped in myself, trying not to hurry too much. There was silence for the next two minutes and I began to wonder if I had made an ass of myself. Sergeant Thomas's head appeared over the top of the turret. 'Here, Evan,' he said, 'what are you skulking in there for, man? If you stop digging every time a bit of shit comes over, we'll never get finished. Come on out of it, now, and do a bit of bloody work. There's no reason to hop in the turret every time you get a bit of shit thrown at you.' 'All right,' I said, giving in to Sergeant Thomas's greater experience, 'get out and do some more digging.' Evan and I climbed out on to the engine plates at the back of the tank and prepared to drop to the ground. But with a scream and a crash another shell arrived. Something glanced along the side of my boot and two or three more pieces hit on the tank with a clang. Evan rolled sideways off the back of the tank and fell to the ground. 'Are you all right?' I asked him. 'Yes, sir.' 'Well get back in the turret, I'm not going to muck about digging in this stuff.' To my considerable satisfaction, I heard Sergeant Thomas also ordering his men to take cover: he was not going to recant entirely, however, but made them lie under the tank and begin to scoop a trench there. As I started to climb up on the tank again, I put my hand on one of the two-gallon water containers on the rack behind the engine. It was still very

hot from the heat of the exhaust. I climbed back on to the turret
and said to Evan and Mudie: 'I'm going to make some coffee
from the hot water at the back of the tank. You can stay there if
you like, but I'm going underneath at the back.' Evan remained
inside, muttering something about not sticking his bloody neck
out, but Mudie and I were underneath the rear end of the tank
before the next shell arrived. Here we lay, drinking warm, if
somewhat silty coffee, while the shelling continued irregularly –
it was a solitary mortar which plagued us – for the best part of an
hour. In one of the intervals I took a mug of coffee up to Evan,
although I didn't wish him luck with it.

Andrew came back from the Colonel's tank and sent me over
to it to do a spell as duty officer during the night. I rolled up my
bedding, humped it on my back, and followed his directions
until I saw the great bulk of the Grant in the increasing moonlight. John Simpson of 'B' Squadron had arrived there on the
same job, and I felt happier at seeing someone I knew. He was
still the youngest officer in the regiment after two and a half
years' commissioned service, a very tall, slim, young gentleman
whose conversation was often informed with an entertaining
sarcasm. He made some polite remark about being glad to see
me back, and began to tell me that he had been 'spending the
evening in injecting morphia into our supporting infantry', most
of whom, by his account, had crowded into the turret of his
Sherman when the shelling started. The greater part of the shells
had apparently landed among the infantry vehicles and heavy
tanks at the back of the leaguer. 'My tank is now a dressing
station,' he said, in a mock-serious voice which, so carefully did
he maintain it, made it clear that it was an insurance against real
seriousness. Although at the time it seemed to me – and I think
to all of us – that we were behaving with admirable restraint,
afterwards I realized how obvious that restraint would have been
to anyone who, like a film audience, could have taken a detached
view of us. In Sergeant Thomas's voice saying: 'There's no
reason to hop in the turret every time' there was a higher, more
excitable note, an exaggeration of the usual Welsh singsong. In
ordering Evan and Mudie back into the cover of the turret, I had

enforced my order with two or three redundant blasphemies. And now John and I continued in this awful vein of banter as we went to look for a place to put our beds.

There were one or two German infantry positions and pits for vehicles to be driven into: beautifully finished and deep-cut trenches. John selected a deep narrow trench about the length and width of a bed, and was going to drop his blankets into it when I said: 'I think there's some stuff in the bottom of it.' 'Oh!' John peered down into the murk. 'I hope it's not a corpse.' That was exactly why I had said 'some stuff' instead of 'something'. But the object, whatever it was, was as long as a man and in a pose which suggested limbs. I stretched a tentative and reluctant hand down into the pit, wondering whether I should touch a stiffened arm, shoulder or leg. I had aimed at the centre of the mass to avoid contact with the face and teeth. Of course, after all this agony it was not a corpse, but someone else's bedding. We had been forestalled and had to sleep in a more open pit dug for a small truck.

When we had arranged our beds I walked back with John to his own tank. It was nearly double the size of my own, and impressed me that evening, seeing a Sherman at close quarters for the first time, as a massively safe stronghold. In a few days' time I would not willingly have changed my low-built and comparatively fragile Crusader for it. On the side of it was painted a huge eye. 'The eye of Horus,' said John. 'He's the nearest thing in Egypt to the God of battles. I put it on with sump oil and the black off a brew-tin.'

We found two infantrymen still sheltering in the turret, although the shelling had been over more than an hour. One explained quite lucidly that he was keeping the other company; his companion he explained being 'took real bad'. This I thought at first meant seriously wounded, but he was apparently suffering only from shock. We found a truck to take him to the M.O. and he was helped out of the turret, and lowered down the front of the tank, shivering and moaning. The oblivion induced by John's morphia seemed to have left his head and nerve centres but not his limbs, which refused to support him. The infantry sentry who helped us get him down, disdaining John's device of banter, said honestly and plainly to me, 'I'll be glad when this is over, won't you, sir?' While this was not a very clever thing to say, it was exactly what I was thinking, and I agreed with him sincerely. The exchange of banalities did us both good.

By the time John and I had got back to our beds, and had settled down, after sharing a packet of chocolate, the British twenty-five-pounders, spaced every twenty-five yards behind us, had opened a barrage lasting several hours. The noises of the shells, just as the noises of aeroplane engines, varied according to the angle at which they struck the ear. One gun which appeared to be firing more or less directly overhead sent a shell which whistled. Possibly at some part of the night there was some German counter-battery fire, or some heavier guns of our own joined in. At all events, there was every variety of noise in the sky, a whistling and chattering and rumbling like trains, like someone whispering into a microphone, or like the tearing of cloth. The sky was lit up almost without pause by the tremendous flashes on the horizon, and the noise was so continuous that we slept easily beneath it. Once I woke, providentially, in time to prevent the driver of a fifteen-hundredweight truck who had wandered into the area, from taking us and the pit in his stride.

As duty officer, with the last spell of duty – four o'clock until dawn – I had to wander about the area, visiting the various guards and pickets, deal with any messages received over the air by the duty operator, call the Colonel at five o'clock, and then rout the whole regimental group out of bed. The infantry had a machine-gun post out in front of the leaguer, which reported snipers out to their front. The fifteen-hundredweight which had almost run over me in bed had been one of a unit which had leaguered in front of us and had been withdrawn through us after having several casualties from these snipers. While I was talking to this picket, two bullets sang past in the darkness like innocuous insects; one struck a tank somewhere and rebounded whining into the darkness.

At five o'clock I woke the Colonel, who lay in his opulent sleeping-bag, in his pyjamas, his clothes and suede boots neatly piled beside him; a scent of pomade drifted from him as he sat up. I told him the time and about the snipers, and handed him over to his batman who already hovered behind me with a cup of tea. I went about stirring the sleeping cocoons of men with my foot. On the way I woke John and said, 'Have some whisky. I suppose we've sunk pretty low, taking it for breakfast.' Unfortunately there was no more chocolate.

By six o'clock the wireless in every tank was switched on, engines were running, and at six-fifteen, through a thick morning mist, the Crusader squadron began to move out in close formation ahead of the regiment. Andrew had relayed rather vague orders to me: but the only thing that seemed clear to me was that there was now no one between us and the enemy. If that were so, it seemed crazy to go swanning off into the mist; but I was fairly certain it was not free from doubt, because I knew there had been a traffic of one or two vehicles passing through our lines in the early morning – and they were soft skinned vehicles, not tanks. Presently, as I moved slowly forward, keeping one eye on the vague shape of Andrew's tank in the mist to my left, I saw on my right a truck, with its crew dismounted. I reported it to Andrew, and cruised across to investigate it. It was, of course, a British truck, whose driver told us there was a whole unit of soft vehicles ahead of us, and as far as he knew, no enemy in the immediate neighbourhood. There was no more mention of snipers, and I imagined these would have been part of some kind of patrol who had now returned to their own lines.

Andrew now began to call me impatiently over the air: 'Nuts five, Nuts five, you're miles behind. Come on. Come on. Off.' Speeding up, we saw the shape of a tank looming ahead of us again, and made for it. As we came nearer, it was recognizable as a German derelict. I had not realized how derelicts can complicate manoeuvres in a bad light. We increased speed again; but there seemed to be no one ahead of us. I began to suppose we had passed Andrew in the mist, and realized that we were lost, without any information of our position or objective. In fact, the regiment had made a sharp turn left while we were halted, and if Andrew had mentioned this to me over the air we could have found them easily. As it was, we continued to move vaguely round until the mist cleared. Seeing some Crusaders on our left when it grew clear enough to pick up objects at a distance, we approached them: they belonged to one of the other regiments in the Brigade, and had no idea (although their colonel was in one of the tanks) on which side of them our regiment was moving. How all this came about I am not sure, because I afterwards found Brigade and regimental orders to be very clear, and there was never an occasion in later actions when every member of a tank crew did not know what troops were on his right and left. This was, however, only the third time the regiment had ever seen action as a tank unit, and I was probably not so far behind the others in experience as I felt.

Meanwhile we rushed eagerly towards every Crusader, like a short-sighted little dog who has got lost on the beach. Andrew continued to call up with such messages as: 'Nuts three, Nuts three I still can't see you. Conform. Conform. Off.' I perceived that two other tanks of the squadron had attached themselves to me and were following me slavishly about, although the other tank of my own troop was nowhere to be seen.

Another Crusader several hundred yards away attracted our attention, and we rushed towards it, floundering over slit trenches and passing through some of our own infantry. As we approached another trench, I was too late to prevent the driver from running over a man in black overalls who was leaning on the parapet. A moment before the tank struck him I realized he was already dead; the first dead man I had ever seen. Looking back, I saw he was a Negro. 'Libyan troops,' said Evan. He was pointing. There were several of them scattered about, their clothes soaked with dew; some lacking limbs, although no flesh of these was visible, the clothes seeming to have wrapped themselves round the places where arms, legs, or even heads should have been, as though with an instinct for decency. I have noticed this before in photographs of people killed by explosive.

The Crusader which had attracted our attention was newly painted, covered with bedding and kit: tin hats and binoculars

27

hung on the outside of the turret, and a revolver lay on the turret flap. Although it was outwardly undamaged, we saw that it had been abandoned. As my own field-glasses were old and quite useless, I told Evan to get out and bring the ones hanging on the derelict. He was very reluctant. 'It might be a booby trap, sir,' said he, rolling his eyes at me. This seemed unlikely at that stage of the battle, and I said, not very sympathetically, 'Well, have a look first and make sure nothing's attached to them. And if nothing is, get them.' Very gingerly, he climbed on to the other turret, and returned with the glasses. While he was getting them, I had at last caught sight of the regiment, and we moved across to them, with our two satellites.

We took position on the right, the Crusaders still lying in front of the regiment, and my own tank being near a derelict Italian M13, apparently no more damaged than the tank we had just left, and covered with a camouflage of scrub. Two burnt-out German tanks stood about fifty yards apart some four hundred yards away to our right front. The other Crusaders were spaced out away to the left of us and over into some dead ground. Nothing seemed to be happening at the moment of our arrival.

I had a look through my new field-glasses: they were certainly an improvement on the ones that had been issued to me. I thought I could make out some lorries and men moving about on the far skyline, and reported them. Two or three other tanks confirmed this and said they could see them too. Unfortunately, our R.H.A. Battery, which had been withdrawn for barrage work, was not yet back with us and these vehicles were out of range of our seventy-fives and six-pounders. So we continued to sit there. Evan produced a thriller and found his place in it. Mudie asked me to pass him a biscuit. I took one myself, and cut us a sliver of cheese each from the tin. I took off my greatcoat and draped it over the turret. We seemed to have settled down for the morning and I began to wonder when we should get a chance to brew up.

I was disturbed from a mental journey through the streets of Jerusalem by the shriek and crash of a shell which threw up dark grey smoke and flame near one of the heavy tanks. During the next hour these shells continued to arrive, with the same tearing and shunting noises as I had heard the night before. Among them, however, was a disturbing new kind of explosion, the air-burst, which the 88 mm. gunners often fired for ranging and to make the occupants of open tank turrets uncomfortable. By tinkering with their fuse they produced a sudden thunderclap overhead, which, beyond drawing a straight line of tiny puffs along the sand, hardly showed after the moment of bursting: so that the first time I heard the bang I was unable to find a dust cloud anywhere to account for it.

The flashes from these guns were not visible: they continued firing spasmodically for about two hours, distributing their fire between the Crusaders and heavy tanks. After a time they began to introduce some sort of oil-shell which burst with a much greater volume of flame and of black smoke. One of these set fire to the bedding strapped to the outside of a Sherman, but the crew soon extinguished this and climbed into their tank again. Apart from this short interlude of excitement, shells continued to arrive and to miss, and we to sit there in sulky silence, reading our magazines and books, eating our biscuits and cheese, and indulging in occasional backchat over the air, for the rest of the morning.

About midday, feeling that the futility of war had been adequately demonstrated to me, I arrived back among the supply vehicles, to refuel. We seized the opportunity to have a brew-up, and ate some of our tinned fruit. An infantry sergeant and three or four men had brought in a German prisoner, a boy of about fifteen, who looked very tired but still defiant. He had remained lying in a patch of scrub while our tanks passed him, and after the supply echelon had arrived, dismounted, brewed up, and settled down to wait for us to come back to them, he had started to snipe them. The sergeant, who regarded this as an underhand piece of work, was for executing the boy at once. 'Shoot the bugger. That's what I say,' he kept repeating. His more humane companions were for giving the prisoner a cup of tea and a cigarette, which he obviously needed. I think he got them in the end.

Having refreshed ourselves and our vehicles, we went back and sat beside the camouflaged derelict again. Presently an infantry patrol, moving like guilty characters in a melodrama, came slinking and crouching up to my tank. A corporal, forgetting his attitude for the time being, leant against the tank, saying: 'You see them Jerry derelicts over there, them two?' He indicated the two burnt-out tanks to our right front and added: 'They've got a machine-gun in that right-hand one. We can't get up to them. They open up on us and pin us down, see?' 'Well, what would you like us to do?' 'I should have thought you could run over the buggers with this,' he said, patting the tank. 'Well, we'll see. I'll have to ask my squadron leader.' I indicated his tank, 'Will you go over and tell him all about it?' 'Very good, sir,' said the corporal, suddenly deciding that I was an officer. He departed. His patrol, who had been slinking aimlessly round in circles, waiting for him, tailed on behind him.

Andrew's instructions were of the kind I was beginning to expect from him. 'See what you can do about it. See if you can get those chaps out of it. But be very careful. I don't want you to take any risks.' I interpreted this to mean: 'If you make a mess of it, I wash my hands of you,' and opened the proceedings by ordering Evan to spray the area of the derelict with machine-gun fire.

The machine-gun, however, fired a couple of desultory shots, and jammed; Evan cleared and re-cocked it. It jammed again. A furious argument followed, Evan maintaining that the trouble was due to my not passing the belt of ammunition over the six-pounder and helping it out of the box. I pointed out that the belt was free on my side. Our understanding of each other was not helped by the fact that while I was speaking into the i/c microphone, Evan removed his earphones because they hampered his movements. He then shouted to me, disdaining the microphone, words which I could not hear through my heavy earphones. At length the conversation resolved itself into a shouting match. Evan became more and more truculent, and I ordered the driver to begin advancing slowly towards the enemy. This had the effect I wanted. Evan stopped talking, and applied himself feverishly to mending the machine-gun. After about a hundred yards I halted and scrutinized the derelict through my glasses. I could see no movement. I wondered what the crew of the machine-gun felt like, seeing a tank slowly singling them out and advancing on them. Evan was stripping the gun in the bad light and confined space of the turret, skinning his fingers, swearing and perspiring. At this moment Andrew's voice spoke in my ear, saying airily that he was going to refuel: 'Nuts five, I'm going back to the N.A.A.F.I. for lemonade and buns. Take charge. Off.' So now I was left to my own devices.

Looking down for a moment at a weapon-pit beside us, I

saw a Libyan soldier reclining there. He had no equipment nor arms, and lay on his back as though resting, his arms flung out, one knee bent, his eyes open. He was a big man: his face reminded me of Paul Robeson. I thought of Rimbaud's poem: 'Le Dormeur du Val' – but the last line:

Il a deux trous rouges au côté droit

was not applicable. There were no signs of violence. As I looked at him, a fly crawled up his cheek and across the dry pupil of his unblinking right eye. I saw that a pocket of dust had collected in the trough of the lower lid. The fact that for two minutes he had been lying so close to me, without my noticing him, was surprising: it was as though he had come there silently and taken up his position since our arrival.

Evan's swearing approached a crescendo. 'I'll have to take the bastard out,' he said. 'It's the remote control's bust. I'll fire it from the trigger.' We got the biscuit tin off the back of the tank and mounted the gun on it loose, on the top of the turret. From this eminence, as we advanced again, Evan sprayed earth and air impartially, burning his fingers on the barrel casing, his temper more furious every minute. At length he succeeded in landing a few shots round the derelict tank. A red-faced infantry subaltern ran up behind us, and climbed on to the tank. He put his hands in his pocket and pulled out two grenades, the pins of which he extracted with his teeth. He sat clutching them and said to me: 'Very good of you to help us out, old boy,' in a voice much fiercer than his words. We were now only about thirty yards from the derelict, and saw the bodies of men under it. They did not move.

'There they are!' cried the infantryman suddenly. A few yards from the left of the tank, two German soldiers were climbing out of a pit, grinning sheepishly as though they had been caught out in a game of hide and seek. In their pit lay a Spandau machine-gun with its perforated jacket. So much, I thought with relief, for the machine-gun nest. But men now arose all round us. We were in a maze of pits. Evan flung down the Besa machine-gun, cried impatiently, 'Lend us your revolver, sir,' and snatching it from my hand, dismounted. He rushed up and down calling 'Out of it, come on out of it, you bastards,' etc. The infantry officer and I joined in this chorus, and rushed from trench to trench; I picked up a rifle from one of the trenches and aimed it threateningly, although I soon discovered that the safety-catch was stuck and it would not fire. The figures of soldiers continued to arise from the earth as though dragon's teeth had been sown there. I tried to get the prisoners into a body by gesticulating with my useless rifle. To hurry a man up, I pointed a rifle at him, but he cowered to the ground, like a puppy being scolded, evidently thinking I was going to shoot him on the spot. I felt very embarrassed, and lowered the rifle: he shot away after his comrades as though at the start of a race. I began to shout: 'Raus, raus, raus,' with great enthusiasm at the occupants of some trenches further back, who were craning their necks at us in an undecided way. Evan unluckily discouraged them by blazing off at them with a Spandau which he had picked up, and some high explosive began to land near the tank, which was following us about like a tame animal. Evan now found a man shamming dead in the bottom of a pit and was firing at his heels with my revolver, swearing and cursing at him. Another German lay on the ground on his back, occasionally lifting his head and body off the ground as far as the waist, with his arms stretched stiffly above his head and his face expressive of strenuous effort, like a man in a gymnasium. His companions gesticulated towards him and pointed at their heads, so that I thought he had been shot in the head. But when I looked more closely, I could see no wound, and he told me he was ill. Two of them assisted him away.

From the weapon pits, which were crawling with flies, we loaded the back of the tank with Spandaus, rifles, Luger pistols, Dienstglasse, the lightweight German binoculars, British tinned rations and the flat round German tins of chocolate.

As the main body of the prisoners was marched away under an infantry guard, the high explosive began to land closer to us. I did not feel inclined to attack the further position singlehanded, so I moved the tank back and tacked it on to the column of prisoners. The mortar stopped firing at us, and some of the infantry climbed on to the tank to ride back. I reported over the air that we had taken some prisoners.

'Nuts five, how many prisoners?' asked what I presumed to be Andrew's voice. 'Nuts five wait. Off.' I said, counting, 'Nuts

33

five about figures four zero. Over.' 'Bloody good. Most excellent.'
Apparently it was the Colonel talking. 'Now I want you to send
these chaps back to our Niner' – he meant the Brigadier – 'so
that you'll get the credit for this.' This was unfortunately more
than my conscience would stand. I felt that all the work had been
done by Evan and the infantry officer, and said so. This was a
bad thing to say to Piccadilly Jim, because it showed him that I
did not agree with him about snatching little gobbets of glory
for the regiment whenever possible. The infantry were in
another Brigade, as Piccadilly Jim knew. Evan said: 'You were
a bloody fool to say that, sir. You've as good as thrown away an
M.C.' I said shortly that if I had, it was an undeserved one.

The reaction on me of all this was an overpowering feeling of
insignificance. I went over to the infantry officers who were searching the prisoners and said: 'You did most of the dirty work, so
you'd better take them back to your Brigade.' The one who had
ridden on my tank replied. 'Yes, we had orders to,' in such a
supercilious way that I almost decided to insist on my right to
escort them after all. The man with a bad head was lying groaning on the ground. He clutched his head and waved it from side
to side. I think perhaps he had ostitis: the pain made him roll
about and kick his legs like a baby.

The turret, after the removal of the Besa, and our leaping in
and out of it, was in utter confusion. During our struggles with
the machine-gun the bottom of an ammunition box had dropped
out, and the belt of it was coiled everywhere. The empty belt
fired from the biscuit box mounting had fallen in whorls on top
of this. The microphones, spare headphones, gunner's headphones and all their respective flexes were inextricably entwined
among the belts. Empty cartridge and shell cases littered the
floor. On the surface of this morass of metal reposed the Besa
itself, and an inverted tin of Kraft cheese, which had melted in
the sunlight. I rescued a microphone and a pair of headphones,
and got permission to retire and reorganize. On my way back I
was to call at the Colonel's tank. This I duly did, but my ears
were singing so loudly that I could scarcely hear his kind words.
As soon as the tank moved away from the prisoners, we were

again fired on by a mortar, which followed us as we moved back, dropping shells consistently a few yards behind us. We brewed up in dead ground to the enemy behind a ridge; the mortar continued to search this ground with fire, but never got nearer than thirty yards, and that only with one shot.

We examined our trophies, and were shocked to find that the infantry had stolen all our German binoculars while enjoying our hospitality as passengers on the tank. We all bitterly reproached them, and I regretted ever having wished to give them extra credit. We had left, however, a large stack of machine-guns

Making a fire in a petrol tin.

and rifles, which we dumped. Three Luger pistols, which we kept: these are beautiful weapons, though with a mechanism too delicate for use in sandy country. There were a few odds and ends of rations, cutlery, badges, knives, etc., which we shared out, eating most of the extra rations there and then in a terrific repast, with several pints of coffee. At last I decided we ought to rejoin the squadron, and reported we were on our way back.

After we had been back in our position about a quarter of an hour, someone on the right reported twelve enemy tanks advancing. A second report estimated twenty. Soon after this a very hot fire began to fall around us. Two petrol lorries were hit at once and began to blaze. The Germans came towards us out of the setting sun, firing, and supported by anti-tank and high-explosive fire. Some of the Crusaders, Andrew's tank included, began reversing. I moved back myself, but it was obvious that we should soon get moved up with the heavy tanks. I halted. Someone could be heard calling for smoke. Andrew was rating the squadron for bunching up and his own tank meanwhile avoided reversing into a Grant more by luck than judgement. There was a certain amount of incipient panic apparent in some of the messages coming over the air. The enemy fire grew more intense: it seemed incredible that only the two lorries had so far been hit. I crouched in the turret, expecting at any moment the crash which would bring our disintegration, seeing again the torn shell of the tank we had passed the previous evening – it seemed weeks ago. I could not see the enemy tanks any longer, and was not sure after so much reversing and milling around, exactly what the situation was. These were the intensest moments of physical fear, outside of dreams, I have ever experienced.

Control now instructed us: 'Open fire on the enemy. Range one zero zero zero. Give the buggers every round you've got. Over.' With, I think, some relief the various squadrons acknowledge. 'One O.K. off'; 'Two O.K. off'; 'Three O.K. off.' I ordered Evan to fire. 'I can't see a muckin' thing,' he protested. 'Never mind, you fire at a thousand as fast as I can load.' Every gun was now blazing away into the twilight, the regiment somewhat massed together, firing with every available weapon. I crammed shells into the six-pounder as fast as Evan could lay and fire it. Presently the deflector bag was full of shell cases, and Evan, who had now adjusted the Besa, blazed off a whole belt without a stoppage, while I tossed out the empty cases, too hot to touch with a bare hand. The turret was full of fumes and smoke. I coughed and sweated; fear had given place to exhilaration. Twilight increased to near-darkness, and the air all round us gleamed with the different coloured traces of shells and bullets,

36

brilliant graceful curves travelling from us to the enemy and from him towards us. The din was tremendously exciting. I could see a trail of machine-gun bullets from one of our heavy tanks passing a few yards to the left of my tank, on a level with my head. Above us whistled the shells of the seventy-fives. Overhead the trace of enemy shells could be seen mounting to the top of their flight where, as the shell tilted towards us, it disappeared. Red and orange bursts leapt up beside and in front of us.

Darkness ended the action as suddenly as it had begun; the petrol lorries alone blazed like beacons, answered by distant fires in the direction of the enemy. Gradually we found our way into leaguer, creeping past the beacons after the dim shapes of our companions. My first day in action had been eventful enough: I felt as if I had been fighting for months.

I shall remember that day as a whole, separate from the rest of my time in action, because it was my first, and because we were withdrawn at two o'clock that morning for a four days' rest. We arrived about four o'clock and lay down to sleep at once. My last sensations were of complete satisfaction in the luxury of sleep, without a thought for the future or the past. I did not wake until ten o'clock next morning, and when I opened my eyes, still no one was stirring.

5

We were out of battle for four days, resting and doing all the small jobs which have to be done as soon as a regiment comes out of action even after so short a time as twenty-four hours. A Crusader, for instance, had run over some wire in the dark, and in the morning we found some forty yards of rusty Dannaert spikes and coils wound round the sprocket between the track and the side of the tank. This wire took two days to remove, although it was probably collected in about two minutes. The light metal mudguard had to come off: the track itself to be broken and the sprocket to be slowly turned over, in short bursts of two or three turns, for hour after hour, while a gang of fitters hauled at the wire, cutting it off with wire-cutters as it came away. Everyone's fingers were lacerated, and under those conditions it was certain that at least half of these scratches and cuts would turn into desert sores, messy and painful wounds which are hard to heal even when you can keep them clean.

Several officers and men who had been slightly wounded in the first actions came back to us while we were resting. 'A' Squadron began to look like a squadron again, although the promised new tanks did not come. Edward and Tom arrived together in a jeep, Tom with his filthy pipe and rakish air of being in the know, common to many people who live among horses; Edward full of polite pleasure at finding me back, overwhelming me with enquiries about myself, and answering my descriptions with incredulous exclamations. 'Really? *No.* Did you? How perfectly terrific, etc.' exactly as if he were still at a garden party, where presumably he learnt this kind of repartee. He cleverly seemed to ignore what was said to him, having, I suppose, evolved this protective barrage of small talk against effusive acquaintances at home. For Edward is what is called in our current idiom 'a social type'. Unfortunately this inability to pay attention hampers him in action, where he often sits in his tank with the earphones on and doesn't hear what is said to him at critical moments. That fault was one I had still to discover.

Before I left the regiment to do camouflage work, eight months before, Edward had already begun to lean upon Tom in most matters of squadron government. Tom had the silver tongue often attributed to a good horse dealer: for him, blarney had long been a science, and when we were all second-lieutenants, Tom was already talking others into dependence on him, while the rest of us were conscientiously calling everybody Sir and keeping notebooks in which we recorded the size of our men's feet. Tom had very soon learnt the names, nicknames and history of all the men in the squadron who were popular and influential in the men's or N.C.O.s' messes. He had sold horses to the Colonel before the war, so that he was not in the position of an ordinary second-lieutenant, the little boy who has to be seen and not heard. All this would probably have made us dislike him out of jealousy. But he was never sycophantic, and he took a pride, as he once told me, in knowing the right way to talk to everyone, so as (in his phrase) to get them eating out of his hand. Even so, although I liked Tom, I did sometimes resent him walking in over our heads. After all, many of us had more commissioned service than he had, before we came to the regiment.

Another person who came back to the regiment from the left-out-of-battle camp, was Raoul, who had come out on the boat with me, a curious person with interesting antecedents. He fiercely resented Tom's success, as he fiercely resented at least half the circumstances of his life everywhere. He was the son of a British officer and a Frenchwoman, and had been brought up in France on books and no games at a Lycée until, when he was fifteen, his father being dead, he quarrelled with his mother and ran away to sea. He went to South America and back on an oil tanker, and on his return, still not too fluent in English, joined the Royal Tank Corps as a trooper. After three years in the British Army, he had learnt to speak English and to use five or six times in a sentence the only swear word ever employed by most regular soldiers (and one, incidentally, which must be understood to punctuate most of the direct speech in this account). He had discovered himself to be irresistible to most women. At the outbreak of war he decided to apply for a commission, which he obtained about eighteen months later. In spite of all this experience he had little idea how to deal either with his superiors or his inferiors, and was the most unpopular officer in the regiment. He foolishly used to run down the Yeomanry by comparison with the R.T.C., in his objectionable, too audible voice. This, combined with his curious origins, accounted for the disapproval of the majority of the officers whose origins and ideas were beautifully standardized. He swore at all the men under him and never remembered, when he was satisfied, to tell them so. This was chiefly a sort of protective, hedgehog attitude acquired because he was in fact too shy and sensitive to have run away from a rich home and thrown himself on the world's mercy. He had never found his balance. I had begun by disliking him as much as anyone, but as I began to understand him, having been given the clue to his character by his history, I found him likeable and well meaning. He was now pleased to find me with the regiment again. 'You're the only person who'll be glad to see me,' he said, characteristically, and added, seeing Tom and Edward pass: 'Look at Tom, I suppose he thinks he's second-in-command of the Squadron. Well, if they make him a captain over my head I'm bloody well going to leave the regiment.' I was able to divert him into reminiscence about some girl in Alexandria.

I have lumped together these three sketches of people, because when you know something about them, and about the personal situation between us, it will be easier to see how we behaved as we did in and out of action during the next few weeks.

Our last evening before going into action again was a busy one. In the morning, a church service was held by the padre: everyone who could spare the time came and stood round him, while he intoned two or three collects, and hymns were sung to the lugubrious accompaniment of a saxophone. The padre had an ascetic appearance and an accent which owed more to his public school than to his clerical studies. He had a somewhat halting delivery, particularly when reading or quoting. But there was no humbug about him; he was there to give some help, and he persuaded everyone that what he said he believed. As the last unmelodious words of the ragged hymn lost themselves among the metallic noises of preparation, and the priest raised his hand, looking like one of the Brangwyn murals in Christ's Hospital chapel, to give the blessing, out stepped Piccadilly Jim, occupying the last few moments, though with bowed head, in giving a last twirl to his moustache and regarding his suede boots. The laces of these boots were tied in reef knots, with exactly equal ends hanging symmetrically on each side of the foot, ending at the welt of the boot. 'Tomorrow,' he said, 'we shall go forward to fight the second phase of the battle of Alamein. The first phase, the dislodgement of the enemy from his position along the whole of his line of battle, is complete. In that phase this Division, this Brigade, did sterling work. The Divisional General and the Brigadier are very pleased.' Here he interposed some acknowledgement to the efforts of individuals, somewhat like an author acknowledging indebtedness in a preface, adding: 'But you all did your jobs, in a way of which you can be proud. In the action at dusk on Tuesday, you stuck to your guns, you didn't give way, and you were extremely successful. When it was possible to investigate the position it was found that we had knocked out five enemy tanks, without casualties to ourselves, and at the price of one lorry. That was most excellent. Bloody good. Couldn't be better.

'Now this time, in the second phase, we shall not have quite so much dirty work to do; other people ... er ... are to be allowed to look in. General Montgomery is going to divide the enemy's forces up into small pockets. Tonight the New Zealanders will attack and after them will go the Ninth Armoured Brigade and other armoured formations. When General Montgomery is ready we shall move in behind them, to administer the *coup de grâce* to the German armour. That is a great honour and you can take credit to yourselves that it has been granted to this Brigade. When we've destroyed the enemy's armour and routed his forces, we shall then go back to Cairo, and ... er ... have a bath, and leave the other buggers to do the chasing for us.'

This speech, the first of Piccadilly Jim's résumés I had heard, impressed me without deceiving me. It was couched in a nice mixture of parliamentary and colloquial terms, magnifying what we had done, half belittling what remained to be done, half glorifying it. And ending with a seductive rumour of leave, which he was certainly not entitled to offer us. It was exactly the right speech, in exactly the right words. It put everyone into a good fighting temper, likely to last them throughout the next week of action.

As soon as we had dispersed, the less exhilarating facts crowded upon us. New tanks were due to arrive and must be taken over. The reassembly of the suspension on the tank which had run across some barbed wire was not complete and would have to be completed by night. Every tank must be filled with food, rations, current and emergency, water and ammunition. Lorries jolted and lurched slowly round from tank to tank, distributing their wares; one petrol, another oil, another water, and at length the quarter-master, ready for once to hand out socks, battledress, greatcoats without even taking a signature for them; and the ammunition lorry, which threw us out a pile of shells in cardboard cases. We stripped off the cardboard and the safety clips on detonators and filled the racks with bright brass shells, resting on their wasp-coloured noses. Flaps had to be torn from the M-G ammunition tins, and the belts inspected to see they had no rounds loose or projecting. Grenades were to be primed.

Inside the squat, angular, sloping turrets the gunners were busy fitting back the dark blue steel-jacketed machine-guns, oiled and spotless, and replacing the great sliding breech-blocks of the six- and two-pounders: loosening the ammunition in the racks. The operator, crammed in the top of the turret, tested the metres on his set, breathed and hummed into the microphone, listening for sidetone, tried a remark to the gunner over the inter-communication. And the driver, busiest of all, at each tank was now outside, tipping in great tins of petrol and oil, wrenching at the fan belts with a spanner, levering and sweating to tighten the tracks; now inside, making the engine roar, watching his gauges.

Myself and all the other troop leaders rushed from tank to tank of our troops, to the squadron leader to report each tank ready to move, to receive final orders and draw in with china-graph pencils on our cellophane map-covers, the outline of the New Zealand 'Box', the route of the advance Armoured Brigade, the known positions of some mines and enemy anti-tank guns. Then this information must be given out to troops. At the last hour of twilight it appeared that the oil lorry had contrived to pass one of my tanks by. I staggered off into the murk and found the fitters, from whom I borrowed a fourteen-gallon drum. But to carry it back by hand and search for the right tank among all the indefinite shapes of vehicles was obviously foolish. I put it down and looked about for a vehicle to do my portage. The only one available was a jeep, to which at the moment no one laid claim. In this, carrying the drum of oil, I set off, only to drive almost immediately into a slit trench. This necessitated sweating about to find a three-tonner or a tank to tow us out. Sending the jeep-driver to arrange matters with the fitters (when I had located them again) I went back to explain the delay to Edward. Here I found Andrew beside himself with fury, who rated me violently for not carrying the drum by hand. It appeared he was to navigate the regiment next morning in the jeep. He spoke as if I had lost the jeep on a mine and as if on him personally depended the regiment's fate. In fact, our path into action lay along very clearly defined tracks which every man in the regiment had had pointed out to him on his platoon commander's map. A child could have found its way into that battle; the same is true of most battles. Andrew's remarks were not quite ridiculous enough not to infuriate me, however, in my harassed state, so I left him to swear at the air and went back to work. In five minutes we had the jeep out of its hole and in a quarter of an hour had delivered the drum and brought the jeep back to Andrew whom I saluted smartly, omitting, since he would be using it before first light, to tell him about the pool of oil on the passenger's seat.

It was now about midnight; we were to move at four o'clock, and prepared to get some sleep, since every tank in the squadron was now topped up and fitted with everything down to boiled sweets, condensed milk and coffee from an opportune mobile canteen. But we were hardly between the blankets before our ears caught the unmistakable rumble of Crusader engines. The new tanks, long despaired of, were arriving. During the next hour came four of them. This necessitated a complete revision of the composition of troops and the provision of crews for the new tanks, whose skeleton delivery crews returned to their delivery point. N.C.O.s acting as gunners or drivers were promoted to tank commanders. Changing tanks about meant hasty unstrapping of kit, redistribution of rations, particularly the canteen stuff, and a frenzied search for more maps, which had to be marked. All this in darkness.

The arrival of the new tanks utterly altered the geography of the area. Having grown used to recognizing each tank by its distance from the next and by the direction in which it faced, a man sent from one side of the area to the other in the dark had to contend with the sudden apparition of tanks where none had been before. This caused immense confusion. The wirelesses in the new tanks had to be checked and netted on the regimental frequency. One of the tanks allotted to me had a wireless out of order. A spare part had to be found and fitted: at first the wireless mechanic shut himself in the turret and worked with the light on: but this was soon forbidden because light streamed out through cracks between the two halves of the turret-top. After that he worked by touch. The new tanks were deficient in ammunition, petrol, oil, water and internal fittings. They had no tommy-guns in them, no bivouac tents strapped along their sides. Their tracks wanted tightening. Their machine-guns were half-hidden in a paste of dust and oil, in which they would have to stay, since to strip them in the dark would only result in the loss of all the essential small parts. The delivery of these tanks at this hour and in this state was nothing in the least unusual: it would not be too much to say it was typical. The cause of it, as of most military and civilian confusion, was lack of imagination, this time on the part of the people behind the line, who never troubled to find out what happened a few miles in front of them. As a result of constant journeys to and fro across the area of men laden with burdens of all kinds from small wireless parts to tins of cheese and bully beef, all four new tanks moved with us in the morning at the appointed hour, although not in a condition to inspire their weary crews' confidence.

The move up to our battle positions was the usual tedious grind along powdery tracks; wireless silence was in force. The crews mostly sat bunched in the turrets, smoking, chewing sweets or biscuits, reading when it was light enough, or when an easy-going tank commander would allow the turret lamp to be switched on. The noise of engines prohibited casual conversation. Those who had nothing to read slept uneasily, huddled up like birds. Troop leaders leaned anxiously on their turrets, feeling the last of the night air against their cheeks. The dust caked on everyone's face who looked out of his turret, and on the drivers, on whom so far the greatest strain fell, who drove straining their eyes at the dustclouds, their armoured flaps open. Later, the crews' turn comes, and the drivers sit for hours perhaps, over books. The unnatural loudness of our voices over the intercommunication prevents any conversation from being companionable or comforting by this, the only audible method. There is no knowing what thoughts may come during these approach marches: they are the only moments when it is hard to avoid reveries, and they take place during the last and most depressing hours before dawn.

6

As it grew light the head of the column swung through half a right-angle, and we saw ahead a gap with barbed-wire walls, bearing metal triangles attached to the wire, the gap through a minefield. Here we passed, craning our heads in a momentary interest, three monstrous tanks, the first Churchill tanks we had ever seen. They were being sent into the battle on test: unfortunately, whoever arranged these tests sitting safely behind a cavalry moustache and a desk in G.H.Q., Cairo, had omitted to inform the combatant troops, and one of the three was destroyed neatly and ruthlessly by our own anti-tank gunners. For the moment, however, there they were, a side-show for us to gape at as we swung past and into the minefield.

It soon appeared that the attack of the night before had not been entirely successful. We had to deploy for action immediately on emerging from the minefield. We had heard that the plan for the preliminary attack by New Zealanders, Highland troops, and tanks, had made provision for one hundred per cent casualties, provided that the objectives were taken. It was soon apparent that these casualties had been more easily fulfilled than the condition of taking the objectives. We passed an area of weapon pits where British and Italian corpses lay together: it was not easy to see them through the dust. A tank action was in progress about four hundred yards in front and to our right. The regiment wheeled right and halted, with a screen of Crusaders in front. In the no-man's-land area ahead of us a Daimler scout car, flying a red cross, was moving and halting, moving and halting, collecting wounded out of holes in the ground. We moved forward, looking across a great plain. Vehicles of some sort could be made out on the horizon, but out of our range. Raoul and his troop were sent still further out and reported enemy tanks. Presently these tanks advanced and we all fired at them. I now had a new gunner, called Kerr, having a voice exactly like Mudie and hailing also from Glasgow. Unlike Mudie he had a respectable appearance and did not talk much. He seemed to be an inexperienced gunner, and did not do much harm, except with one lucky shot which hit and set on fire one of the enemy. His other shots fell short or plunged over the target. Two more of the enemy were set on fire and the others retired. We began to creep forward, swinging west again to face the enemy. As we advanced, I remembered how we had sat so long during my first action within a stone's throw of enemy infantry, and I began to look very carefully at the trenches we passed. About two hundred yards from the German derelicts, which were now furiously belching inky smoke, I looked down into the face of a man lying hunched up in a pit. His expression of agony seemed so acute and urgent, his stare so wild and despairing, that for a moment I thought him alive. He was like a cleverly posed waxwork, for his position suggested a paroxysm, an orgasm of pain. He

seemed to move and writhe. But he was stiff. The dust which powdered his face like an actor's lay on his wide open eyes, whose stare held my gaze like the Ancient Mariner's. He had tried to cover his wounds with towels against the flies. His haversack lay open, from which he had taken towels and dressings. His water-bottle lay tilted with the cork out. Towels and haversack were dark with dried blood, darker still with a great concourse of flies. This picture, as they say, told a story. It filled me with useless pity.

As the tank went gruffly past, the head of a living man was raised from the next pit; he had not strength to keep it raised, but lifted head and arm alternately, as a man lifts a hat on a stick to draw fire. As we went on moving past, an awful despair settled on his face. I halted the tank, realizing suddenly that the driver had not seen him, and had the engine switched off. I got out of the turret and ran to him, hoping there were no snipers about. I held a two-gallon water can for him while he drank the warm, rusty water. Then he said: 'Can you get me out of here?' He was a second-lieutenant, I think of New Zealand infantry. His leg was hit in several places below the knee, and covered, like the dead man's wound, with a towel. 'The one that got me got my water-bottle,' he said. 'I've been here two days. I've had about enough. Can you get me out?' his voice broke and hesitated over the words. He suddenly added, remembering: 'Do something for the chap in the next trench,' and seeing my face, 'is he dead?' 'Dead as a doornail,' said my voice. The words blundered out without any intention. God knows what made me say them. I had meant only to nod. I saw him wince and felt dumb with embarrassment. 'He was hit the same time,' he said. 'Three Jerry tanks came almost up to us, firing at you, I suppose. Your stuff was landing all round here.' I went back to the tank, not quite sure if Piccadilly Jim would allow this diversion, and asked permission to take a wounded man back to an R.A.P. on the tank. In my fear of a refusal, I made my request too long-winded, so that Piccadilly Jim replied: 'Yes, yes, yes, yes, yes. But for Christ's sake *get off the air*. I'm trying to fight a battle. Off.'

47

I went back to the trench and said: 'Could you manage to get on the back of the tank if we help you?' I began to feel ashamed of having the protection of a tank for myself. 'I can manage anything to get out of this bloody pit,' he said, and we hauled him up on to the hot steel plates above the engine, while he clenched his teeth and shut his eyes, but made no complaint. Our long hesitation at this spot had been remarked by the crew of an enemy mortar somewhere, which began to lob shells in our wake as we moved back, luckily quite inaccurately. We dumped the wounded subaltern and his kit and equipment, about which he was very anxious, among a guard set over some prisoners, who were already giving him hot tea as we skidded round to face the enemy.

We had hardly rejoined the squadron when the whole regiment moved back to refuel in the area where we had deployed in the morning. A desultory high explosive fire made the refuelling an uncomfortable time. The squadron officers held a sort of hasty conference in the lee of Edward's tank, ducking solemnly behind it at each ominous whistle, and waiting silently for the shellburst as a sort of permission for whoever was speaking to complete his sentence. To us, N.C.O.s came saluting (out of habit rather than from any punctilious instinct) and reporting the usual defects already acquired in spite of all the maintenance of the last few days. Few Crusader tanks would run for more than two days in action without developing either an oil-leak or a water-leak. Two tanks, one of mine and one of Raoul's, now had oil-leaks, which would mean them going back to Light Aid Detachment workshops, now established at the mouth of the minefield. I was to go back to L.A.D. in charge of these two tanks, Raoul having demanded permission to stay in action. Tom came across and joined the group, puffing at his foul old pipe. 'Some bastard of a sniper got poor little Bingham and Corporal Wood,' he said. Edward said, 'I'm very sorry,' but, having to think in terms of tanks, asked, 'Was the tank damaged?' 'No, he just plugged one of them while he was looking out of the turret, and I suppose the other one looked out to see what it was and he got it in the neck too. I'd like to catch the sod that did it. Poor little Bingham. One of the best little operators in the squadron.'

I was ordered to take over the tank of these unfortunates, which had been driven back to L.A.D. and was waiting there. Late in the afternoon we arrived back at L.A.D., where, as we halted, the tall Ordnance officer whom I had first seen on my arrival at the regiment on Boat track, approached, saying: 'Just disperse a bit, will you, old boy. We've only got thin skins here, you know, and they've chucked quite a bit of stuff at us already.' 'What's the trouble?' 'Oil leaks, these two. Have you got a sound Crusader here? One that had a couple of chaps sniped in it?' He hesitated. 'It's O.K.,' he said. 'But the turret's in a bit of a mess.' I was afraid it would be, but obviously we should have to make the best of that. As we walked over to find it, the L.A.D. officer shouted after me. 'I say, if you're taking that tank, will you put your own driver on it? The other chap's a bit shaken up, and I think he could do with a rest.'

We found the tank; its driver was leaning against it eating meat and vegetables out of a tin. His mug stood on the front of the tank. He did not appear very shaken: a young North Country-man, stocky built with a square red face and tow-coloured hair. 'I didn't seem to be getting any orders, like, sir,' he said, in explanation, 'so I had a look at George – Corporal Wood. He were sitting in his seat and at first I thought he were all right. But then I see he were dead. Then I had a look at Bert, like, and *he* were all over blood; so I come out of it jildi.'

The inside of the turret confirmed his story. The breech of the six-pounder and its deflector bag, the wireless, the machine-gun, and the shells in the racks were splashed thickly with blood. A bloody belt hung from the machine-gun; the empty cases of some shells lay in an inch-deep pool of blood on the floor. It would not have required much imagination to see a steam of blood rising. 'Bit mucky in the turret,' said the driver, as though apologizing to an inspecting officer, when I climbed down.

There was not much daylight left, and I got permission over the air to stay out of battle for the night and come back in the morning. The night was cold and noisy; I scraped myself a shallow trench beside the tank and slept in it wearing all my clothes and my British warm, rolled in my blankets and the remains of an Arab coat of lambswool. My tummy was full of hot tea and tinned Maconochie. For some time I was worried by a regular whistling of projectiles overhead from some British gun, and lay watching the usual parabola of machine-gun bullets climbing towards Orion and falling away. This night, like every night of that battle, was one of clear starlight. At length, reassured by the stars, and generating warmth inside my wrappings, I slept.

In the morning we spent a little time in cleaning up the guns and ammunition of the tank we had taken over, and switching on the wireless, could hear the conversation of the regiment moving up into battle positions from its harbour. When all the kit was transferred from our old tank we set off between nine and ten o'clock to rejoin the regiment. The bodies of some Italian infantrymen still lay in their weapon pits, surrounded by pitiable rubbish, picture postcards of Milan, Rome, Venice, snapshots of their families, chocolate wrappings, and hundreds of cheap cardboard cigarette packets. Amongst this litter, more suggestive of holiday-makers than soldiers, there were here and there bayonets and the little tin 'red devil' grenades, bombastic little crackers that will blow a man's hand off and make a noise like the crack of doom. But even these, associated with the rest of the rubbish, only looked like cutlery and cruets. The Italians lay about like trippers taken ill. The plumed helmets of the Bersaglieri were everywhere, fluttering in the breeze of early morning; many of the plumes had already been torn off to decorate the petrol lorries and ration trucks.

On the air I heard Raoul's voice reporting the position of an 88, Edward adjuring him to be careful. A few minutes later, Raoul's jubilant report of the gun's capture. The Colonel's congratulations, closely followed by the Artillery O.P.'s voice announcing more 88 positions. Edward's message, 'Nuts three, Nuts three, be careful. Don't go swanning over that ridge,' was not acknowledged.

By now we were moving about in rear of the brigade trying to find out which flank the regiment was holding and soon we discovered the Colonel's tank and the heavy squadrons, while about a mile away could be seen the Crusaders crawling about on a ridge, where already the burnt-out remains of some other regiment's Shermans lay where the German guns had caught them the day before. Moving across towards the heavy tanks, we passed the body of a Highland infantryman, whose legs with their red hackles were doubled under him, broken at the knee. I afterwards heard that he was found to have been attached by the Italians to a bursting charge, which the R.E.s neutralized. This was typical of the behaviour of the little beasts, who combined underhand cruelty with cowardice, and servility when we caught up with them. The Italian attitude of 'we never wanted to fight' was true enough, with its corollary: 'We only wanted to tie bombs to wine-bottles and corpses, and leave them for you to find.'

I reported to the Colonel, and moved out to join Edward. I was beginning to have trouble with my trousers, an outsize pair of issue Battle Dress, which I had hastily confined under a belt. They began to escape the belt and slip down; as fast as I pulled up one side the other descended. In despair I undid them and put them on again from the beginning. This activity was too much for the two remaining fly buttons, which came off: we used to think it typical of military methods that Battle Dress trousers are supplied with sharp tin buttons which begin cutting themselves off as soon as they are sewn on.

I met Edward's tank coming back past two burnt-out Italian M13 tanks, whose crews were neatly laid in two charred rows beside them. For some reason the feet and boots had nearly all escaped the flames. I dismounted and went across to Edward to get some verbal instructions and save pattering on the air. 'Raoul's been hit,' he said; 'tank brewed up and his driver's killed. Ken Tinker's bringing him in. He *is* a bloody fool, he would go over that ridge. . . . Go on up to somewhere where you can see, will you, and take charge of the squadron till I come back.' I went up as far as I could and stayed watching the 88s which were firing across my front. I heard the Colonel ask the

R.H.A. to get on to a 'suspicious object' on the ridge, but did not realize until the ranging shells arrived that I was the suspicious object. I retreated protesting over the wireless and soon afterwards the Colonel's tank moved up near me and he beckoned to me to dismount and come across to him. I tumbled out of the turret, forgetting the state of my trousers, which immediately fell round my ankles. I hauled them up with one hand and staggered across to him. When I had told him all I knew I hobbled back and climbed on to my tank in time to hear Ken Tinker reporting the destruction of the last 88.

In the afternoon we moved right-handed to the North and tried to drive the enemy gunners from a track, visible on the skyline by the tops of its telegraph poles. During the afternoon my wireless set gave out and breakdowns among the remaining tanks reduced the Crusader Squadron to three tanks, with one wireless between them. Edward, in the tank with the wireless, with Tom as his gunner, lay low in a gully about a thousand yards from the 88s on the track. His gears were not working well and he didn't want to move more than necessary. Away to the left a sergeant in the other 'dumb' tank stayed put, hull down, observing. By shouting directions to my driver above the noise of the engine (internal communication having broken down with the wireless) I was able to move my tank, using dips in the ground to within about 660 yards of the telegraph poles, and saw that two or three Mk III tanks were in support of the guns. When I had seen as much as I could, I turned my tank and moved back into Edward's little wadi, where I dismounted and ran across to his tank. I made two of these journeys, and Edward passed back my news to the regiment over the air. Each time I dismounted I still skidded about on the metal of the tank, the soles of my boots being covered with half-congealed blood from the pool in the bottom of the turret. Flies hung above the tank in a cloud.

Towards the end of the afternoon smoke projectiles, spluttering smoke along the whole arc of their flight, began to come from the direction of the telegraph wires. We had still moved no nearer, and were more or less pinned. We all looked expectantly and apprehensively at the smoke, expecting an attack of tanks or infantry. But none came: this was our first experience of one of the enemy's favourite tricks. The smoke cleared away. Some of our heavy tanks began to lumber closer to the Crusaders, like clumsy yokel spectators. They immediately came under heavy fire from the 88s, who ranged on them with grey bursts of HE, and a few earsplitting airbursts to keep the crews' heads down. I looked across at Edward and Tom, who were peering anxiously over the tip of our little depression, pipes clamped in their mouths, and puffing out sharp spurts of smoke through their lips as though they were opening fire.

Presently the chukkering noises in the air announced that the 88s had got their range and were loading with armour-piercing shot. Three of the big tanks were hit almost simultaneously and the aviation petrol in them went up with a whoosh. Out of the turrets tumbled their crews, pursued by volcanic tongues of flame and billows of black smoke. The crew of one of them huddled together, supporting each other like revellers going home. The shells flew over one after another.

Glancing over the side of my tank I saw a magazine, oil-stained and torn, but with a familiar cover; it was a copy of *Esquire*. The Crusaders had not moved and remained turret down, unnoticed by the enemy gunners: I decided to get out, and did so, landing full upon the magazine as another round rocketed overhead, and adding a bloody footprint to the stains of oil and wet sand. In the turret the gunner and I turned the pages, and admired with as much attention as we could the pink Petty girl, telephoning from her cushions, and a full page of colour photography, depicting various Hollywood personalities dining and dancing at some club or other. Beneath the oil stains their white tuxedos and seductive dresses shone, and they flashed their red lips and white teeth at the photographer. As we turned the page on a Peter Arno roué, the twenty-five-pounders began to reply, and Piccadilly Jim's voice sounded in the earphones, addressing the heavy tanks, which had begun to move back in the face of a murderous fire: 'Nobody told you to retire. Get back. Bloody well GET BACK and give the buggers Hell. You're bloody sticky.' The tanks stopped edging away and came up into their positions. The twenty-five-pounders found the range and the enemy gunners began to limber up and get away soon afterwards, leaving two guns and their crews behind destroyed. We saw no more of their tanks and soon after this I was sent back to refuel. The petrol lorries had arrived beside a derelict fifteen-hundredweight truck, the driver of which lay half in, half out of it, with one leg almost entirely torn off. The battledress serge had peeled away, showing a wreckage of flesh and the ends of bones. We moved some little distance away from this sight, and began to bang petrol tins about, tearing them out of their wooden outer cases, and bashing holes in them with an Italian bayonet. As soon as we had finished filling up the tank, we got a brew on, of coffee and M. & V. and as we were about to decant the silty coffee into mugs and mess tins, heard another tank coming. We looked up casually enough, since the engine note was that of a Sherman, and we were not much interested in the other squadrons. What we saw was an odd sight. It was a Sherman, right enough, but as it came towards us in the beginning of twilight, a red aureole about the turret top proclaimed

that the inside was blazing. The immediate effect was of something supernatural, as though the dead or mangled crew were bringing in the remains of their tank. A very slim connexion reminded me momentarily of Ambrose Bierce's Horseman in the Sky.

The tank stopped about a hundred yards off, as I finished my coffee, and a figure emerged from the driver's manhole and came a little unsteadily towards our fire. It was Nick, a lieutenant out of 'C' Squadron whom I had only once met before, at Division when he was sent up there on a liaison job. His pleasant face was as black as a Christy minstrel's and lit up into a nigger smile as he said: 'Hullo old boy, I've just brought my Sherman in; I wonder if you'd mind giving a hand to put the fire out?' and sniffing – 'I say, is that coffee?' We poured him out what was left, and went round to collect fire-extinguishers from the two petrol lorries. Armed with these, and our own, we approached the burning tank, a little gingerly perhaps, since we knew that there were thirty or forty high explosive shells and thousands of bullets inside the burning turret – enough to blow the whole tank to pieces, and fill the air with random pieces of metal for twenty minutes afterwards as the ammunition in the belts went off. We began by pouring all the water in the tank's water cans into the turret. The fire within retaliated with a frightful hissing and sparks flew up among a fog of steam and oily smoke. But the fire was undiscouraged. It had now spread to the driver's seat in spite of this. The tank engine had continued running for the two miles or so necessary to bring it in – one of those things which happen, but of which no one demands an explanation. The fire-extinguishers had more effect, and the fire died down to a smoking mass. We had untied the kit bags from the kit rail on the outside of the tanks and carried them and the blankets to a safe distance, where they were piled. We were not disposed to waste any more of our water, and all the extinguishers were squirted dry; so we climbed down off the hot shell of the tank and went back for another brew of coffee. Twilight was now deepening into darkness, and the skyline where the battle had taken place was punctuated with the gleam of three of our

Shermans, still blazing merrily. We heard through the earphones dangling on the side of the tank the regiment receiving orders to move back into leaguer. 'Lot of muckin' good it was our trying to put that out,' said someone. The red glow was visible again in the turret of Nick's tank. Among all these beacons, we thought our small brew fire might be allowed to break the rule against fires after dark. The enemy were at least four miles off, anyway, and no one fires at a solitary camp fire, except with small arms. But the M.O., very agitated, arrived in a scout car and remonstrated with us. As the second brew of coffee was ready, we gave in to him and put the fire out, further stopping his mouth with a cup of coffee.

That night we were issued with about a couple of wineglasses full of rum to each man, the effect of which was a little spoiled by one of our twenty-five-pounders, which was off calibration, and dropped shells in the middle of our area at regular intervals of seconds for about an hour. The first shells made a hole in the adjutant's head, and blinded a corporal in B Squadron. I spent an uncomfortable night curled up on a bed of tacky blood on the turret floor.

7

The next morning we struck westwards again, and crossed the line of telegraph wires without seeing any of the enemy. Within ten minutes of crossing we picked up a deserter, who said they had withdrawn a long way to the west. His news was treated with suspicion and we went on as cautiously as before. But the country was flat for some miles, and only on the horizon could be seen the beginning of some ridges, among which the tail of a dive-bomber stuck straight upwards, a tiny arrow in the earth. Scrutinizing these distant things, I only looked down just in time to see that my driver was heading for a deep pit, dug to hide a lorry in. I turned him hastily on the edge of it, but the wall gave way beneath the Crusader's 18 tons, and we slid in, almost overturning the tank and snapping one of the tracks, which had already done well over their mileage, and were more or less worn out. I was delighted to say good-bye to this tank and change into a clean one, one of those which had had minor breakdowns the day before, and which our L.A.D. had dealt with. We came up to the line of the high ground without further excitement, though we put a six-pounder shell across the bows of one of the 11th Hussars' armoured cars, which had moved out well ahead of us, and was under suspicion of being an enemy vehicle. We had aimed well ahead of it, and the effect was immediate. It came tearing towards us like a scalded cat and drew up alongside. Its commander, a sergeant, leaned out and said 'Was that you firing at us?' We admitted it, and apologized. 'With that?' pointing to the long snout of our six-pounder. 'Well, yes,' we admitted. 'Phew!' he said. 'Don't do it again, please.' He moved out ahead of us again.

The 88s were waiting for us as we came abreast of the crashed Stuka, and their grey bursts and ricochets came bouncing round us and the armoured cars, who scuttled back to our line. Between the armoured cars, the Crusaders, and the O.P. we brought the twenty-five-pounders down on them, and destroyed one. The others limbered up and pelted away behind their tractors, across the plain, pursued by our shells. Edward's tank broke down near here and another of the N.C.O.'s tanks. We were left with two Crusaders and the American Honey tank belonging to the R.H.A. Orange Pip, which Edward mounted. Tom was in the other Crusader and we spread ourselves out, watching the horizon and the flanks: the regiments on our right and left had been more cautious, and had not kept up with us. Presently Crusaders came creeping up on our right and left. Tom went back to the aeroplane to get some petrol from a lorry which had come up. The O.P.'s tank was about a hundred yards to the left of the plane, and I about three hundred yards ahead of it. Through my glasses I saw the squat shapes of enemy tanks coming over the horizon to our front. I counted twelve of them, in groups of three, four or two. They were well out of range but coming towards us fast, for every time I looked away and back again they were larger. They ran into a belt of heat haze and began to shiver and stagger, becoming shapeless and blurred. 'Nuts

57

three, have you seen these tanks in front of us?' I asked Edward. 'Yes,' said Edward. 'Have a shot at them if they come within range. Over.' 'Nuts three O.K. off.' We waited. Evan, who had now come back to me as gunner, went on reading his novel inside the turret. He had taken his earphones off, as usual, and had not heard my conversation with Edward. I let him go on reading; no point in waking him up until they got nearer. The Crusaders of our flanking regiments had seen them now, and began shuffling back to a position on the high ground about a mile behind us. Evidently they did not feel very comfortable on open ground. Nor did I; but there was no reason to move yet. I looked back at Tom's tank and saw that he was rummaging in the Stuka's cockpit. His crew were sitting on the ground, smoking; so they had not seen the enemy either. I began to wonder if it was all a mirage, and seeing the other regiments had now withdrawn, reflected that I must be the foremost tank of the Eighth Army at the moment. Probably I was, for the majority of the Armour was out of battle that morning.

When the enemy seemed to me to be about two miles off, I called up Edward and asked permission to have a crack at them at extreme range. 'Nuts three, O.K.,' he said. 'I'll observe your shot. Tell me when you're firing.' I called Evan away from his novel and made him look out of the top of the turret. 'I want you to have a crack at one of those tanks. The centre of those three just by the patch of scrub will do.' 'They're not tanks, sir,' he said immediately; 'they're trees.' 'Don't be bloody silly. What do you think trees would be doing in the desert?' 'They're not tanks, sir,' he repeated stupidly. 'Well, I don't give a damn what they are, fire at the centre one by the patch of scrub.' I slammed a shell into the breech, contriving to skin my fingers, as usual. I tapped him on the shoulder. 'Loaded. Put maximum range on and fire when you're ready.' I looked up as the breech leapt back and the empty case tinkled out. Seconds passed in suspense. The mushroom of dust grew silently out of the ground hundreds of yards short. 'No good,' I said. 'Wait.' I reloaded. 'Nuts three, that one was short. Pitch 'em up. Over,' said Edward over the air, somewhat redundantly. 'Three O.K. off.' The blurred shapes

58

continued to enlarge. 'Evan,' I said presently. 'Have a look at those trees now. Grown a bit, haven't they?' He did not answer; but was so struck with the force of this demonstration that he immediately pulled the trigger and the recoiling breech hit me a grand crack on the elbow. Luckily my arm was free to move and was thrown back violently with no more than a bad bruise. I called him a clumsy mucker and reloaded with one hand. After three or four more shots, all short, the blobs on the skyline began to diminish again and soon disappeared entirely. Tom's tank came grinding up on my left. I trotted over to him and said, 'Well, you lazy old devil. I've just beaten off a massed tank attack while you were grubbing for loot.' 'So I saw,' said Tom, puffing amiably at a German pipe with which he had replaced the breakage of his own. 'There's some mail for you. Pol lorry's got it.' I shouted and signalled to Evan to turn the tank and hopped on the outside of it to guide the driver back behind the Stuka. While they were filling up I read a postcard from Mother and a couple of airgraphs from Diana. I never had more welcome letters. We had a mug of tea and went back to our position.

8

Orders came soon afterwards to rally on a track about six miles back and we moved back at full speed. Here we found the whole Brigade drawing up in column, ready to move on Mersa Matruh and cut off the retreating enemy. A Stuka raid on the rear of the column made a great deal of noise but caused no casualties. We leaguered at sundown in three long rows of squadrons, long enough to brew up and replenish with petrol, oil, water, and ammunition. The scheme was that we should move all night in three columns, nose to tail. But it was a pitch dark night; and though we afterwards did move at night a much greater distance and under almost worse conditions, at this stage of the battle we had not enough experience to do it: after messing about half the night and moving about a mile we gave up, closed down wirelesses except for one set per regiment and, posting guards, the Brigade slept. By first light we were on the move, our own

Crusaders slipping out to the front and flanks of the Brigade. I now had a full troop of three tanks. Edward back in a Crusader, travelled in front of the column with Andrew, who had materialized from somewhere or other, and a new officer known already as 'The Professor', going into action in a Crusader for the first time. Tom, the R.H.A. O.P. and my own troop lay echeloned out along the length of the Brigade's right flank. The country was flat and we kept up a good speed. The flanking Crusaders moving at times more than 30 miles an hour. We had hardly got under way when Tom flew off at a tangent, throwing up billows of dust, after three Italian lorries full of troops. He captured two and was disarming them as I caught him up. The third was getting away but we were recalled by Piccadilly Jim, who was a little amused and much in sympathy with our ardour. 'You'd better let that one go to ground,' he said. 'We'll soon find it again.' And we did. The Crusaders, like enough to hounds, raced across the plain, bellies to the ground, and put up small parties of the enemy every few minutes. Gun crews frantically trying to get their guns and vehicles away, infantry surrendering, lorry drivers – all Italians – driving themselves and their comrades to meet us and surrender. The first of these Italian lorry convoys had driven into our leaguer the night before, eight ten-tonners, crammed with men, with an armoured car of the 11th at the nose and another at the tail of the column. We continued to move across the plain at top speed, and in high glee, elated with all the excitement of the hunt. At these times the Crusader is at its best. The low chassis and long sloping lines give a spectator the impression of a speedboat; the driver and gunner in the turret sway slightly like a speedboat's crew, as they cross the undulating waves of ground.

We took prisoner twenty engineers under a rather arrogant young lieutenant, who chased them into ranks and shouted commands at them before saluting pompously. They had all smashed their rifles. I suppose he did it all very correctly. We searched them and collected some cameras, badges and letters; in half an hour or so 'B' echelon lorries came up to take them back. We set out to find the rest of the column which had moved on out of sight. As we flew across the ground, eyes still skinned for bodies of the enemy ready to surrender, all the anxiety of the previous days of battle gave way to the exhilarating sensations of sport. Suddenly we came upon a veritable house, standing in its own patch of green, shaded by trees. We neared this, the first indication that we were approaching the railway and the coast road, very gingerly. But it was quite deserted. We were now in a valley, without a sight of the columns, or of a single vehicle. All I knew was the column's general direction and centre line, which lay on our left, and that one of our lorry columns which we had seen earlier in the distance was moving parallel to us, between us and the sea. Evan became sullen and jumpy, and began to mutter that we had gone too far and that we should find 88s all round us. I told him to keep his hand on the Besa; but he replied sulkily that he hadn't had a chance to clean it since he took over the tank, and that it was jammed. This was true; these tanks had only caught up the column as it was moving off. As we reached the far side of the valley we saw two men running across our front. They seemed to vanish into the earth. All this time we could hear the radio conversation of the rest of the regiment; chiefly, as usual, the voices of the Crusader squadron, who were doing all the work at the moment. I heard Piccadilly Jim telling the Crusaders leading the column to wheel right towards the railway. We could not see the railway yet, but I ran up the northern side of the valley towards the sea. As we reached the top of the valley we could see a long stream of lorries, mostly Chevrolet 3-tonners and 15 cwts, moving nose to tail along beside the railway line below us. I thought they were probably the column which had been travelling to our right, and anyway, seeing no guns among them, I ignored Evan's protests and we slithered down the slope to meet them. What a haul it would have been if they had been Germans, I thought.

We came down beside one of the trucks and moved at the column's speed, about 10 miles an hour, our right track about a yard from the lorry's wing. I looked into the cab, the driver was a German. I saw him a second or two earlier than he saw me. My driver, of course, who was driving blind, by my directions, continued stolidly alongside the lorry. The German glanced casually sideways at us, and away again. Then a terrible thought struck him. All this was comically visible on his face. He looked sideways again, seemed to confirm his worst fears and swerved violently into the railway embankment, jumping out before the truck stopped moving. Men came piling out of the back in colossal confusion. We halted and waited for them to surrender. But our appearance had been too sudden. They were in a panic. The crew of the lorry behind them could not make out what they were doing. Their conversation translated roughly into 'What the hell are you doing?' 'A tank! A tank! English tank?' 'Where?' (unanswered). The other crew became infected. They all fled up the bank towards the sea. This was disconcerting; I felt very annoyed and shouted after them insults and invitations to return in a mixture of English and German. But they would not. I suppose we could have killed a good many of them as they ran, with my revolver and our tommy gun. But this seemed a futile thing to do. They were surrounded and had no rations, and like a few other fighting soldiers I lack the true ferocity of Battle School Instructors and armchair critics. Besides, the whole situation was too ridiculous to attempt to introduce a serious note. We backed the tank and threw a hand grenade or two at one of the lorries without much effect. Then we blazed off at it with the six-pounder at a range of about 20 yards, but appeared to have missed. When we went closer I saw there were three holes as clean as a whistle through the dashboard and engine. In the end we dismounted and tommy-gunned the engines of the three lorries which had halted. The rear vehicles of the column had turned and made off back down the line. Those in front had driven sedately on unaware of what was happening behind them. While they were doing this I had launched frantic wireless messages into the casual conversations still audible from the regiment, begging someone to come and help bag the rest of the lorries. But Edward was talking to his gunner or driver or otherwise distracted and never heard one of my four messages. At last Tom answered: 'Nuts three I heard you. But we can't do anything about it at the moment. We're going to be busy. Destroy what you can and rejoin. Over.' I acknowledged this as the last of the runners were gaining the far crest. After destroying the three vehicles I seized a couple of blankets, of which we were short, from one of the lorries and a kitbag from a pile of them in the back of another, and turned after the tail of the column. But at this moment the microphone went dead and, being still lost, with the consciousness that petrol was running low, I took no notice of two other German vehicles which passed me, and they ignored me; we drove past each other at a distance of about 50 yards. As we crossed the railway line a man who had been hiding the other side of the embankment sprang up and ran across it. Evan fired the tommy gun at him, which was a senseless thing to do. Anyway, he missed him.

As we topped the next rise we saw below us our own twenty-five-pounders and several other vehicles of our column dispersed straddling the railway line. The enemy vehicles must have run into some part of the column. There was a small station there – Galal Station, the name written on a tin plate – and there we halted while I called up Tom to find out where the squadron was. We sorted out the kitbag and an impressive first-aid set which Evan had found, full of bright scissors and instruments. I found clean underclothes, a dark khaki cotton shirt, and trousers of the same colour, apparently brand new, made of very rough cloth and quite well cut, with sloping pockets and a belt sewn in the waist. There was even a metal ring to hang a watch on, with a small pocket for the watch underneath it. I took these clothes and a khaki high-necked jersey, and gave Evan the rest to divide with the driver. They were more interested in badges, combs, razors, haircream, etc., which were all there.

We set off to find some petrol, and while we were filling up heard the battle begin on the air. Several tanks reporting targets, and the Artillery observation officers promising their fire. There seemed to be a great many enemy tanks. The twenty-five-pounders began to fire over the hill in front, and we heard the tanks reporting direct hits of their own guns. Suddenly the voice of some tank N.C.O. who had switched to the A set by mistake, and thought he was still on Internal Communication, broke into the messages, shouting, almost screaming. 'Bloody good shot! You've 'it 'im. You've 'it the bugger. Go on Lofty, give 'im another. Go on. 'It 'im again' . . . rising to a crescendo. Then the inevitable angry voices of other stations: 'Get on I/C.' 'Bloody well GET ON I/C and look to your BLOODY procedure' (Piccadilly Jim).

Obviously this was a new kind of action; the voices of the participants seemed like those of boys in a shooting gallery. We poured petrol in as fast as it would go, slopping it over the top of the big tin funnel in our excitement and spilling it down the sides of the tank. But long before we had finished filling up some-one's voice in the earphones said: 'They're surrendering.' And we arrived to find the battle of Galal Station over. The regiment had accounted for twenty-seven tanks. A long row of derelict Italian M13s stood by the railway line, some blazing, others apparently undamaged. From one of these I took a small Biretta automatic and its ammunition, as I passed the derelicts to take up my position watching the sea, which I had not seen since leaving Alexandria.

During the afternoon I washed, shaved, and dressed in my new shirt and trousers and the high-necked jersey, tying a blue German handkerchief with a red stripe in it round my neck. Except for beret and boots, the enemy had clothed me com-pletely – and on my belt hung my new Biretta and the Luger I had taken in my first action. When I had completed my toilet, feeling hugely pleased with myself in my brand-new clothes, I walked down to the railway line, leaving a lookout in the top of the tank, to see if I could get another Biretta for Raoul, who would by now be in hospital in Alex or Cairo.

I approached a brand-new-painted M13, with no sign of any damage, from which the crew had apparently fled at the sight of their comrades' discomfiture. There was a promising cask and a sack on the outside of the tank, which we opened. But the cask only contained water, and the sack nothing but little round tins with a smelly Italian kind of bully beef in them. So I climbed on to the turret – the small side doors which stood open on most of the other tanks were closed. I prepared to lower myself through the top. It was dark in the turret, and I leant over the manhole first, trying to accustom my eyes to the darkness and to see if there were any Birettas on the side shelves inside. A faint sweet smell came up to me which reminded me of the dead horse I once saw cut up for our instruction at the Equitation School.

Gradually the objects in the turret became visible: the crew of the tank – for, I believe, these tanks did not hold more than two – were, so to speak, distributed round the turret. At first it was difficult to work out how the limbs were arranged. They lay in a clumsy embrace, their white faces whiter, as those of dead men in the desert always were, for the light powdering of dust on them. One with a six-inch hole in his head, the whole skull smashed in behind the remains of an ear – the other covered with his own and his friend's blood, held up by the blue steel mechanism of a machine-gun, his legs twisting among the dully gleaming gear levers. About them clung that impenetrable silence I have mentioned before, by which I think the dead compel our reverence. I got a Biretta from another tank on the other side of the railway line.

In the evening we closed into night leaguer, facing westwards again. Tom was in high spirits; he and Ken Tinker had found an Italian hospital, and their tanks were loaded inside and out with crates of cherries, Macedonian cigarettes, cigars and wine; some straw-jacketed Italian Chianti wine, some champagne, and a bottle or two of brandy, even some Liebfraumilch. We shared out the plunder with the immemorial glee of conquerors, and beneath

the old star-eaten blanket of the sky

lay down to dream of victory.

The next day, of course, was an anticlimax. We turned west again and made for Fuka, on the last lap to Mersa, from which the appearance of the enemy tanks at Galal had distracted us. Everyone kept his eyes skinned more for loot than for prisoners, and in dismounting to examine the contents of a stranded lorry I lost my Luger, which fell out of my pocket unnoticed. Later in the morning I saw a crate full of Chianti bottles lying in an infantry weapon pit and was for telling my driver to stop and collecting them. But before I could speak he had run clean over them. There was an almighty explosion and the tank lumbered on.

Evan and the driver emerged and jumped to the ground, the driver shouting 'She won't steer.' He had left the clutch in and I jumped down with them, ran round the tank and saw that the track and skirting were blown off one side and she was rolling on the great wheels, from which the solid rubber tyres were blown to shreds, while the sprocket and the other track drove her. In spite of wild protestations from Evan and the driver, Skelton, who had quite lost their senses for the moment, and imagined that to enter the tank was to court death (though if they had been outside it they would have been already dead) – I got in again and switched off the engine. Some sort of light anti-tank gun began firing at us very inaccurately. The shot kicked up the dust short of us, and as I ran about looking at the damage, and back to the big blackened hole where the inviting box of Chianti bottles had been, I was dimly aware of them getting on to us for line and making a huge correction for range with their next shot, which flew well over our heads. I called up Edward and explained what had happened. 'O.K.,' he said. 'Change on to another of your children; can you see what that is firing at you? Over.' 'Nuts three. No. It's solid shot of some kind. Off.' Another tank came up, we flung my kit on it and caught up with the others, who were still advancing.

The gun did not fire again, but we saw vehicles escaping along the top of a kind of sand cliff in front of us. We were switched on to a southerly course by the Brigadier, and climbed on to the plateau, after stalking carefully up on vehicle after vehicle, only to find them burnt-out derelicts. Fuka aerodrome had been evacuated, nothing of any use to us remained, and soon afterwards we crossed the coast road near another landing ground, where the wreckage of a Spitfire lay among that of several Italian and German fighters. There were one or two very well-dressed Italian officers waiting for us, who proved to be the vanguard of that long, straggling column of defeated Italians and Germans

ALAMEIN

which found its own way down to the cage at Fuka. That evening it rained for the first time since the beginning of the battle.

The first downpour took us by surprise and washed most of the victorious feeling out of us. The landing ground became a marsh, and we dried our clothes on the exhaust, garment by garment, and battened ourselves into the turret, where we sat throughout a miserable afternoon, eating wet biscuits and cheese. In the evening I was sent down the road to Brigade in a Marmon Harrington Armoured Car which had been found at Galal. On the way down the dark road we came upon six Germans plodding along by themselves. I sat them on the outside of the car and very reluctantly got out and sat outside with them in the rain. They were dejected and said they had had nothing to eat for two days. I gave them some tins of bully which I had put in my pocket from my tank's ration box, and some sodden pieces of biscuit. We plunged off the road according to our directions, to find Brigade, but were pixy-led by a number of distracting lights and would have spent the night in a weapon pit into which we fell and got stuck, but for the opportune appearance of a stray tank, which obligingly pulled us out. The jerk of being hauled clear threw all the prisoners on the ground, and one of them lost his kitbag, to which he had been clinging as something saved from the wreck. He asked permission to look for it, in a hopeless tone of voice; the tank crew were indignant when I helped him find it and roared off into the murk again.

It was difficult to get rid of the prisoners, but I was determined to find them some food and blankets, because the few people in the regiment who had been taken prisoner and recaptured during the first days at Alamein had been well treated by the Germans. Eventually I dumped them on a guard in the Brigade area whose sergeant had been a prisoner of the Germans for two months and was also well disposed to them.

9

The next morning we went back to the regiment with orders for a move at 8 o'clock, to take Mersa Matruh. 'A' squadron were

strung across the road, my troop combing between the road and
the sea. As we approached an Italian position five men came out
holding up their hands, with packets of cigarettes in them. One
pointed also to his watch, as an inducement to us to take them.
This was very different from the German method of surrendering. They climbed on to the tank and we moved on. But the
main advance had left us behind and when we broke a track
crossing a little ditch, we were stranded out of sight of everyone.
The tank was stuck in the ditch, and before we could mend the
track would have to be towed off it. By now it was about 9.30
and I set out with one of the crew to walk to the road – the other
two members (this was a 4-man tank) staying with the five
prisoners. Luckily we had plenty of rations.

As we walked we built stone cairns on every ridge we crossed,
and after about an hour's walking reached the road, which here
curved away inland, crossing the railway. We passed an abandoned lorry or two, but found no loot in them. The idea of loot
was uppermost in everyone's mind now, and what made us
most impatient to catch up the regiment was the thought that
the others would get to the loot first. An Arab, the first of many,
was already poking about in the back of one of the lorries, and
said to us as we passed: 'Saida. Enta Inglese?' and when we
affirmed this, answered transparently: 'Inglese quois. Alemanni
mush quois. Schwoi biskiert? Sukra? Tsigara?' We gave him a
pack of Italian cigarettes, saying to each other: 'The old bastard.
If we'd been Germans it'd have been Alemanni quois, Inglese
mush quois.'

At the side of the road we waited all day by a stranded Crusader of another regiment. The crew of this tank had a Luger
pistol each and a new type of pistol none of us had seen before.
There was plenty of ammunition, and we began potting at petrol
tins, which entertained us most of the afternoon. This crew
kindly made us some tea and gave us lunch. We picked up some
Italian mess tins and cutlery for eating with from the roadside.

Already a procession of lorries, nose to tail, some of them bearing the Cairo area sign, and all of them patently from base units
– their drivers and crews goggling at everything they passed –

were tearing down the road towards Mersa, with supplies of every kind. There were Air Force ground crews moving up to take over aerodromes. At times the traffic was four abreast as well as nose to tail, and it thickened hourly. A continuous line of abandoned Axis vehicles and tanks, some burnt out but many of them intact, stretched along both sides of the road. Ammunition of all kinds lay about. Hopeful drivers and crews of passing vehicles sometimes got out to poke among the wreckage, but they were too late, nothing had been left for them. One of them was thrilled to find a dead man wrapped in a blanket and submerged in a puddle. During the day hundreds of Axis soldiers came walking eastwards in dejected little groups, not looking at the mass of vehicles bucketing along towards the west, which at times came near to running over them. Sometimes the Italians begged for food. But the Germans went by like sleepwalkers. The few vehicles which tried to beat their way back towards Alexandria were forced off into the sand by the uncompromising stream of supply.

The new type of pistol had jammed; the moving parts had somehow seized up, and we could not make out how to strip it, so I called to four German soldiers who were walking past. They all lifted their heads in apprehension to endure something more. A corporal walked across to them holding the revolver; he could not make them understand what he wanted. When I crossed over and spoke to them in halting German they smiled in huge relief. Only to tell us how to strip the pistol; they had it in bits in a moment, but advised us to prefer the old type of Luger, which was much more reliable. I asked their spokesman, a corporal with two medal ribbons, if they had had anything to eat. He said yes, they had chocolate, and offered us some; they all had ten or more of the round packets of plain chocolate whose empty cartons we had seen so often. We exchanged some tins of bully for some of the chocolate and stood about munching chocolate while the Germans opened the bully and passed it round. A general conversation began. The corporal pointed to the Crusader and inquired: 'Der Panzer ist kaput?' We explained vaguely what was wrong with it; we argued over the relative merits of some Spitfires which roared low over us, and the 110. Photographs were produced. The Corporal had been in France: in Paris – postcards from Paris; in Greece – pictures of the Parthenon. In Russia? No. And how long in Afrika? Vier Monate. They were a Mk III tank crew. Willi, said the Corporal, had only been here sixteen days. Would it matter that he hadn't been issued with a Pay Book yet? Germans set a great store by their Pay Books. Page 4 records all the essential details of their existence – if they lose page 4 they feel they have lost their hold on life. Willi had big ears and looked very like Dopey, the seventh and youngest dwarf. The matter of the loss of his Pay Book had evidently been preying on his mind. I suppose he had been told what an unpardonable crime it was to be found without a pay book – as our recruits are. Poor little toad. So the drizzling afternoon passed, in talk. The Corporal had been at Köln University and had taken part in sports against Cambridge before the war. He said he did not believe in the stories of German atrocities in Poland and Russia – and I don't think he did believe them. Why should he have known anything about them? The whole theory of the German system seems to be that they concentrate their thugs and perverts, and use them apart from their decent fighting men. We heard later from prisoners who had been in Russia how the S.S. Battalions came up to take over the ground won by the fighting troops and to 'deal with' the civilian population. It began raining again and we all sheltered in an old Italian lorry and drank tea. About 5 o'clock an officious staff major in a jeep arrived and ordered the prisoners to be on their way. Presumably he thought we were lowering our morale: strict orders against fraternizing with prisoners were soon published. 'They will only despise you,' said the order. I wonder. At least I got enough material from that conversation for a lecture when the regiment became static again and needed such things to occupy its time. These men seemed to be sure that the campaign in Africa was nearly over – as it should have been after such a victory – and 'Russland auch,' said one of them, 'bringt sich am Ende'. But they all said – as the prisoners in Tunisia told us – in Europe, we should have our work cut out.

The mechanist sergeant of the regiment who owned the road-side Crusader arrived soon after the prisoners had gone. He had seen fit to grow a beard, which none of Piccadilly Jim's men would have dared do, and was unnecessarily dirty. When I asked him if he could give us any help he addressed me offensively as 'My friend', with an evil accent, and refused to do anything for us. As I wore no badges of rank, I could not object to his treating me as he would have treated another rank, but didn't see what right he had to take this tone with anyone, and said so. At the end, towards dark, we persuaded a kindly corporal of the 3rd Regiment in the Brigade to follow our line of cairns across and tow us out. But it grew dark on the way and we could no longer see the cairns, so we passed a very cold night (we had started optimistically in the morning with thin shirts, in sunshine), without blankets, rolled in canvas tarpaulins on inexorably stony ground.

In the morning we located the tank, to my relief, as the corporal had begun to be a little sceptical of its existence, and had suddenly demanded my identity card when we began to lose the cairns. The Italians had apparently been entertaining as well as useful. They were not fighting troops, but the equivalent of an ENSA concert party, and one of them was a padre. They were all very young, and one of them, before the war an opera tenor in Milan, had beguiled the night with what my driver and operator considered 'real high-class music'. They washed up after breakfast and mended our track with great cheerfulness. We gave them a ride to the road, and saw them on to a lorry heading east. We spent another night on the road, and ate a huge supper, having drawn three days' rations for two fictitious stranded tanks from a D.I.D., where I swopped a Biretta for a bottle of brandy. In the morning we caught up with the regiment resting the other side of Mersa, and heard the story of the capture of Mersa, beginning with that of a staff officer going in there in a staff car before the enemy had cleared out and getting put in the bag. The Colonel's tank had been knocked out on the way in; Piccadilly Jim had escaped by the skin of his teeth, but his driver and gunner were killed.

For the moment we were not continuing the advance. Everyone remembered Piccadilly Jim's speech before the battle about leaving the other buggers to do the chasing, and fantastic rumours, called blue lights, began to circulate – the usual one about going home included. 'A' Squadron set going an officers' mess in the back of a 3-ton lorry, and lived on loot. Wine, cigars, cocoa, cherries, chocolate, meat roll and excellent ersatz coffee graced our menu. A great deal of fine white flour went with it, and cherry tarts were on the table four meals of the day. Tom and I and Ken Tinker made an expedition in the neighbourhood and returned with a luxurious black tent, like a sheikh's, for each squadron. Ours had talc windows and even an asbestos flap for leading a hot pipe in. Candles were among the spoil, the tent blacked out completely, and we began to spend convivial evenings.

I took a jeep down to the harbour at Mersa as soon as possible to see if the M.T.B.s were in. Some two or three were there, but not the one we wanted. She was expected in any time, said a rating; and as we stood there she came gliding in with an inward rumble of deep engines and berthed; I saw Norman, browner and more ridiculously muscular than ever, in dirty shorts, and old split gym shoes, shirtless and hatless, emerge on deck. As soon as she was berthed we went aboard. Alec, whom I had last seen just before the ill-fated raid on Tobruk, came out of the poky cabin grinning all over his ugly face, and I introduced Ken Tinker. We all went below and told our news over cigars and orange gin, which they had brought up with them from Alex. Norman wore round his neck a charm I recognized as Milena's. When I saw it, all the pleasant colour of the situation faded, and for a moment I remembered Mila as I last saw her, looking beautiful and clearly bored by my questions, whispering, 'Don't make a scene please, Peter; people are looking at us.' But the atmosphere of bonhomie, gin and cigars soon exchanged the mechanical smile on my face for a real one again. Ken and I drove away in the jeep and rushed to get back in time for tea.

We found Tom very indignant. He had been down to Mersa on a looting expedition with Andrew, had found a lot more cocoa and cherries, and a cask of wine. Andrew had suddenly and inexplicably taken charge of everything, forbidden Tom, nay, ordered him, as Major to Lieutenant, to leave the wine behind, and to hand over to him all the other food so that he 'could see that it was fairly distributed'. At tea Andrew's temper was uncertain and the next morning he announced that we ought to break up the mess, as he had distributed the goods to tanks, and we shouldn't get any in the mess. 'But why didn't you set aside some for the mess?' said Edward. 'You knew we were living in a mess, didn't you?' 'Yes, but you can't go taking it all for the officers,' said Andrew. 'Have you distributed it to tanks?' asked Tom. 'Of course.' 'Well, my crew haven't had any,' said Tom. 'Nor have mine,' I said. 'I don't think mine have, Andrew,' said Edward. Andrew waved a hand vaguely. 'It was there,' he said. 'They probably didn't bother to come and get it.' 'Well, did you tell them it was there?' asked Tom. 'They were told,' said Andrew loftily. We could not understand why and how this situation had arisen; it took us by surprise. No one was sure what to say to Andrew. We were probably relieved when next morning he announced that, since we were (unreasonably, his tone suggested) determined to live in a mess, he was going to live on his tank. And he went. In order to slacken the tension, Andrew was a week or so later transferred to 'B' Squadron, and we began to live in harmony again.

10

When I found out that Division had parked themselves just behind us, remembering my defection, I prepared for a deal of bother. But they made less trouble than I had feared. Their first shot was fired after we had been there two or three days. The Colonel A.A. and Q.M.G., an unpleasant little Welshman whose appearance upheld the theories of British Israelites, sent a note to Piccadilly Jim, saying 'Could you persuade Peter Cameron to pay this mess bill, as all attempts have failed.' This was more subtlety than I should have expected from them. The mess bill enclosed was made out up to the date of my departure from

Division, and had, of course, not been presented to me. Now to send any kind of note to a regimental colonel alleging that one of his officers has not paid a mess bill is a fairly serious charge against the officer. Letting the regiment down, conduct unbecoming an officer and gentleman, and other obsolescent phrases float in the air. I was sent for peremptorily by the adjutant, and protested my innocence. 'You'd better go down and straighten it out with Renny,' said Maurice. Renny was the P.M.C. of the Divisional Messes, a genial, hearty soul whom no one trusted an inch. I took the squadron jeep and drove back into the Divisional area, as one who drives into another century. The atmosphere there was quite unaffected by the battle. Immaculate C.M.P.s saluted and directed me, and I found Renny in his own mess, in the act of drawing off a glass of wine from a huge barrel. 'Hallo, old boy,' he said, beaming. 'Have a glass of this, we managed to get a detachment of C.M.P.s to guard all the enemy foodstuffs and whatnot, so we're well supplied.' This I knew already; Tom and I had been sternly warned off a dump of food by C.M.P.s who were supposed to be 'preventing looting'. I accepted a cup of wine gracefully. 'I came up about a mess bill,' I said. 'There seems to be some trouble. So I thought I'd come up and pay it. Colonel Rickard wrote a note to Piccadilly Jim saying all efforts to make me pay it had failed. Actually this is the first time it's been sent in.' 'Oh, well, there's no hurry, old boy,' Renny replied easily. 'I told Yates to give it to you, but I expect he didn't have a chance.' Difficult to remember that this was the officer who had arranged for me to be sent to Divisional 'B' Echelon at the beginning of the battle. 'I expect you've had quite an exciting time, haven't you?' 'Yes, I suppose I have. Has anyone here noticed my disappearance yet?' I asked. 'I should keep out of the G.I.'s way for a bit. I think Tim Thorpe wanted to see you, or Jim Allett, about your trucks.' 'I'll go along now, shall I?' 'Yes, you'll probably find him in now – A.C.V.6.' 'Thank you for the wine. So long.' I saw Tim about the truck, and he asked me the details of my escape; he said the G.I. was in a fury and sending circular notices to all the departments of the Division to know why I had been allowed to go without his being

74

informed and where I had gone. I paid my mess bill, and finding the Divisional mess as well stocked as if it were still in Cairo area, bought a bottle of Rye and a lot of chocolate and spam, and returned to dinner in triumph. Piccadilly Jim undertook to negotiate with the G.I. and I was allowed to remain with the regiment on condition that I went down to Division again and apologized personally to the G.I. for running away. This was probably going to be embarrassing; but anything was worthwhile in return for my congé. I went down that evening in the jeep. There was only a duty clerk in the A.C.V. The G.I. was in the mess. I went over to the lighted mess tent, and ducked my way into its august company. The General, the G.I. and the G.2., and the Ack and Quack Colonel were playing Bridge. I said 'Good evening', tentatively. The General grunted, either at his cards or at me, and silence fell again. Presently an exquisite young Captain in a tailor-made Barathea battledress offered me a drink. I accepted. The poker sitting seemed to be good for hours yet. I had another drink and discussed some sort of shop with the captain. I don't know what he was; but like everyone at Division he had all the latest news about everything. We were already hundreds of miles behind the fighting line. Tobruk had fallen, and the armoured cars were pushing on to Benghazi. We were out of it; probably going back to the Delta, he said.

Presently the poker players got up to stretch their legs, and the G.I. said to me, rather awkwardly, 'Just step outside a moment with me' – he checked the 'old boy' which from long habit was rising to his lips and said 'Will you, please?' instead. Outside he puffed at his pipe and regarded the stars. We strode up and down in silence. At last he said: 'This business of your running away. Why did you do it?' He seemed hurt. I tried to think of some explanation that he could understand but finally said weakly that I didn't know, and that I didn't think I was much use in 'B' Echelon, driving a two-tonner. 'That's absurd, of course,' he said. 'I never gave any such orders. If you'd asked me, I should have given you permission to go back while the battle was on, willingly.' (Oh, would you? Then why refuse my application when I did ask you?) Aloud I said: 'Well I'm very sorry, Sir.' 'Well,' said the Colonel with a note of relief at having got this awkward business of ticking me off over and done with, 'don't be unmilitary again,' – he permitted himself an 'old boy' – 'you seem to be doing well with your regiment: you'd better stay there.' I was itching to get away, but he added, in the voice of one doing a duty of politeness, burying the hatchet, etc.: 'Come in and have a drink.' So I had to go in again, and everyone except the General spoke kindly to me, though he spoke over my head and across me and broke in upon the conversation as though I was invisible and inaudible. I bade him good night as soon as possible, saluted, and managed to get out of the hut without knocking my cap off.

11

As though to round off this incident of battle, I was sent back to Alexandria in a fifteen-hundredweight the next day to have my eyes tested; for I had lost one pair of my glasses and badly cracked another during the battle. I was given £50 of regimental money and a shopping list like a quartermaster's inventory. We started early in the morning, a tonner sergeant and myself, and began badly by skidding into a three-tonner, on the west road. But we escaped damage and as the sun climbed, the surface of the road dried off. We retraced the steps of the infantry's coastal advance, a long trail of derelicts and scattered debris, ammunition, clothing and equipment, until we bumped round and over the last cluster of shell holes and began to eat the last miles to Alexandria. Presently we passed the Palm Trees and the police post by Burg el Arab and forked left into the outskirts of Alex, as I had done so many times before the attack. We were held up by the tea house and the little bridge at Scots Corner by a long column of prisoners marching, and then entered the stinking Street of the Abattoirs, crossed the great bridge and began to follow the clanging slug-like course of the trams between walls too high and close together to permit of our passing them. The usual cluster of Arabs clung to the back of the tram ahead, grinning all over their filthy faces and alternating the V-sign with gestures begging cigarettes – an innocent stranger might have thought they were blowing us kisses. The men and women on the sidewalks, mostly the poorest of the Greeks who form a great part of the city's population, smiled and cried out to us, seeing our faces, clothes and vehicles covered with dust, and a shrapnel hole or two in the side. Heading for Mohamed Ali square and the centre of the city, I was still debating whether to swallow my pride and go to see Milena, or to put up at an hotel – or even to sleep in the truck, which at the time seemed the most natural of the three. We drove along the Corniche, past bathers and sun-bathers, a blaze of coloured costumes as bright as a garden; at Stanley Bay troops on leave and the huge indolent population of smart women hid the sand and dotted the blue half-circle of sea.

Turning off the main road to Mustapha barracks, and parking the truck and its driver in the transit camp there, my mind was still not made up. But while I cogitated and debated, and talked to Sergeant Norman on the pavement outside Mustapha, about accommodating ourselves, my feet were subtly leading us towards Milena's house in Rouchdy Pasha, and I let them take us there and went in to see who was at home. It was strange to find how easy it was for me to cross the little strip of garden and open the old door with its peeling paint, without the thought much disturbing me, of all the times I had gone there before with an evening of dancing and moonlit strolling before me. The effect of battle had been admirably cathartic. But the odd face, with its delicate bones and nobility of line, the twisted smile and curious sad dishonest eyes; and her sinuous and clearly made body, like a drawing made with an airbrush; her absurd accent; all beat my fortitude down when she confronted me.

Committed now, I took refuge in a flood of my own conversation, telling them all my news, showing them some of the booty, the Luger and Biretta revolvers and the German trousers. They made beds for us in the room above; her mother and father asked me a question or two – the old man, shrivelled and with quick bright eyes, like a lizard even to the lizard's air of ancient aristo-cracy, spoke an appalling English. Her mother, fat, with the blowsy remains of beauty, speaking bad French comfortably.

The wretched little puppy we had rescued from the street and had spent weeks in delousing and feeding up had died while I was away. In the evening Mila, Sergeant Norman and I went to see some film, I forget what it was. Sergeant Norman and I slept on the floor in the drawing room.

In the morning we began shopping in earnest, and bought a great number of tin mugs – M. Pegna taking a day off from his office to come round the bazaars with me and see that I wasn't swindled. I bought six little pewter medicine glasses for drinking whisky. Coming back from the bazaar, I saw a pathetically thin girl in a knitted woollen dress; when we came nearer I was shocked to recognize Titsa. I greeted her and she smiled, not with her usual luminous gaiety, but with an effort. M. Pegna, when I looked round to introduce him, said something about having business at the office and with a flourish of his hat, tactfully left us. I turned round again to Titsa. She had on a knitted woollen dress, made of an appalling green, and grey; in loose, stretchy wool quite unsuitable for any kind of garment designed to fit closely. It had stretched and hung on her, making her look thinner and paler than ever. I asked how she was, and why so thin; she had 'mal à l'estomac' – her mother had been forcing the family to fast again, although their priest had given them a wartime absolution. I steered her into a café and made her take some cakes and coffee – she still refused a meal, and seemed more than usually afraid of being seen out with me by one of her cousins or acquaintances. She reiterated her phrase – 'Il y a du monde.' She wasn't much interested in anything I said, but asked me to take her out in the evening, when she could arrange some sort of alibi for being out of the house.

We said good-bye at Ramleh Station, since she would not go nearer her home with me: and I picked up Sergeant Norman and took the truck down to the docks to see Milena, who was working for Saccone and Speed, selling drinks and tobacco wholesale to ships. We drove the truck into the docks and arranged to fill the spaces under seats, etc., with orange, gin, liqueurs, cigarettes and cigars; sitting on these, we drove out past the sentry and the Egyptian police, congratulating ourselves on getting English gin for 7s. a bottle, and defrauding the Egyptians who had lived upon us so long. In the afternoon we bought some 2,000 eggs from the Nile Cold Storage Company, and a lot of tinned food. The N.A.A.F.I. refused to serve us, because we didn't live in Alexandria, and we finished the day's shopping by ordering 3,000 *petits pains* to be ready, newly baked at 9.00 the next morning. In the evening Titsa and I spent a dismal evening, drinking lemonade in the dark at a café on the Corniche, with the sea growling and stinking like a wildcat a hundred yards away. Titsa went home early, and I met Milena and took her to another film. We went home in a taxi, twined sleepily in each other's arms, as we had often done before, but even in this proximity it was as though there were a sheet of metal between us.

In the morning we started back, after the counting and loading of 3,000 beautiful scented new loaves in sacks. On the way back we stopped at the bulk N.A.A.F.I. at Burg el Arab, which we reached about five minutes after their closing time. A dirty R.A.S.C. corporal, who was in charge of it, refused to sell us any beer, although he had plenty of it, as we could see. We did not much relieve our feelings by suggesting that if the fighting troops were as finicky about their working hours as N.A.A.F.I. employees we shouldn't have begun a battle let alone won it. I should like to have shot him. So although we returned to the unit fully laden, we had not been able to buy so much as a stick of chocolate from the Expeditionary Force Institutes, which are popularly supposed to supply the fighting troops.

We arrived back to find that all the hopes and promises had been dispelled. The brigade was preparing to move forward, up to Benghazi, beyond which the armoured cars were still harrying the enemy's rearguards. Divisional Headquarters was already on its way back to the Cairo area. We were to become part of the famous Seventh Armoured Division, whose sign, the desert rat, was to appear on the mudguards of our vehicles. The tanks were to move by transporter, and another party to go separately by road under the Colonel.

12

I was not much disappointed by this news, and looked forward to seeing the desert in panorama from the back of a transporter. Everyone said that the country near Benghazi was green and beautiful, and I was curious to see the places whose names had been familiar to me before I left England. I also thought of the opportunities there would be to get more loot. We had all seen the enemy so disorganized that it did not seem possible he could regroup enough to give us much trouble. When we heard of North African landings there were very few people who expected more than a few more weeks of mopping up before the African campaign ended. We went forward without any idea of what was still in store for us: when the realization came it broke very slowly, and was cruelly emphasized and re-emphasized.

The transporters arrived, one by one, clanking down the road all day and most of the night – they make the sort of noise one would expect of Vulcan in his forge: it seems too loud to be produced by mortals and terrestrial metals. We did not much look forward to the job of loading the tanks and getting away. Edward, after valiant efforts to overcome an attack of dysentery, had gone into hospital somewhere in the Delta, looking very ill indeed, and Tom, still a lieutenant, was acting squadron leader. We had two new officers in the squadron – Billy, who had been one of the reservist N.C.O.s posted to the regiment, a little dark man with a humorous face and deep lines, almost like scars, round his mouth: and his complete antithesis, Alastair MacCunn, a young smooth-faced amateur fisherman, apt not to speak and to sit about as though he still held a rod. His very appearance is a little like the god of fish described by Rupert Brooke, squamous, omnipotent and kind, if the first adjective may be understood as piscine rather than scaly.

To these we allotted troops. The whole squadron was rationed and drawn up in formations which would get them on to the transporters in the minimum of time. But we knew we had little chance of a smooth working organization. To begin with, the

Colonel had put in charge of the transporter party the squadron leader of 'B' squadron, known to the troops as Sweeney Todd, from his habit of frowning and glaring at everyone, usually without noticing them. Hearing of this choice Tom said: 'H'm. We'll have plenty to do, straightening things out when old Sweeney gets hold of those transporter boys.'

For Sweeney is the true bull in a china shop. Tactless, good-hearted, and perfectly unimaginative, he could infuriate more people in less time than anyone else I know. But all this without the least ill-will towards them, and without a suspicion that all is not well. His lack of imagination makes him shyer than the most sensitive youth: the converse of the man who didn't know much about art, Sweeney likes what he knows, and distrusts what does not come within the range of his experience. Some of the men, who have not much imagination themselves, dislike him and hold old grievances against him, because they have never understood his one complete and unselfish sincerity. Devotion to the regiment. His upbringing as a member of the English upper class seems to have been rigidly typical and has left him with fixed inherited views on life. But if he has the faults of his type, he has its virtues, the famous English virtues of tradition. He is a man who might have stepped from the pages of *Blackwood's Magazine* or *Country Life*. He could tell you how to use an axe or a gun, could discuss crops, blood sports, or livestock by the hour, and has a great love for the English countryside. His favourite reading, I believe, is adventure stories, and the historical plays of Shakespeare. He mistrusts jokes, too many of which he does not understand. When someone makes a humorous remark which escapes him, he looks as unhappy as a great dog who is being laughed at. He enjoyed very much being placed in charge of men and I believe experienced the same sort of pleasure as a small boy who sets out lead soldiers, altering and replacing them exactly to the order he wants. He is afraid of intellectual conversation, of music and of painting.

This was the man Piccadilly Jim had put in charge of the transporter party. In fact he had nothing to do but tell the R.A.S.C. officers the numbers of tanks to be loaded, to see that the tanks were available, and leave them to regulate the whole journey, since the tanks and their crews would merely be loads for the transporters. The R.A.S.C. had never heard of the sub-formations of troop, squadron, etc., and were, quite properly, not concerned with them. There was absolutely no defensible reason why the loaded tanks should travel by troops. If they were unloaded anywhere they could assemble in troops within five minutes. If they were to be loaded by troops the whole system of drawing up troops by transporters must be altered and all these huge unwieldy vehicles moved into a fresh order in the short time before darkness (for we were to start before dawn). Breakdowns on the road would inevitably alter the order again completely. But Sweeney insisted that the transporters must be arranged in the order of troops of tanks. He, and we, by his instruction, ordered the transporters to move. When they began to move, their own officers and N.C.O.s who had not been consulted, ordered them to go back to where they had started. In no time at all a great muddle had been created: the rows of transporters were disorganized, and two Crusaders, in attempts to load them, had snapped their tracks. Into the mêlée rushed a scout car, in which Piccadilly Jim stood, furiously rating everyone who came near him. Of course he found one of the tanks with a broken track, but could not find Tom, and eventually discovered me, and ordered me to put an N.C.O. (who had nothing to do with it) on a charge. Tom and I conspired to forget to do this.

The task of loading a Crusader tank on to the comparatively narrow trailer of a diamond T-transporter, even in daylight, is a formidable one. Two ramps, weighty triangular lumps, are rolled over the end of the trailer and fixed in position making a short, steep incline by which the tank is to mount the transporter. Up these ramps, with perhaps an eight-inch margin of error, the Crusader had to be driven. The tank was lined up and gingerly approached the transporter – the whole incident was like the mating of two immense creatures, mythical and prehistoric, as we saw it in the fading light. The bows of the tank approached the ramps; the tracks, for a wonder, were opposite to them, and it began to move upwards, rearing ponderously. But the driver had misjudged the steepness of the ramps – the tank rolled back and bumped on to the ground, refusing. The second attempt – a rush – carried it full on to the back of the transporter. As the rear roadwheels, churning inside the belt of the track, came upon the ramps, the fore-end of the tank reared fearsomely in the air; a great shape, black against the faintly yellow west. It hung for a moment, as though the eighteen tons of it would turn full over backwards – and then crashed down on to the platform; the suspension softened its fall as the pasterns soften the fall of a rearing horse. It would take a half-hour more to secure it firmly against the jolts of the journey.

We sat down at a table set in the moonlight to our last comfortable supper, and before going to bed, finished the last of our Canadian whisky. Ken Tinker, the R.H.A. observation officer who had been up to dinner with us nearly every evening since we got back to Mersa, had gone back to Cairo with his unit. Tom said: 'I hate going without old Ken. The old lad won't know what to do with himself in Cairo.' He always larded his conversation with these hearty phrases – everyone was an old lad, or a good little chap; Raoul was the only exception. Tom hated him, and did not trouble to conceal this.

We started two or three hours before dawn, trailing down the road with a rhythmic clanking which became a great strain on our nerves before the end of the journey. Among the loot remaining to me was a German inflatable rubber mattress, so far unpunctured. I arranged this with my bedding on the engine plates at the back of my tank above the multiple rear wheels of the transporter, and since the road was reasonably smooth, slept comfortably on until 8 o'clock. I uncovered an eye about five minutes past eight and found the air warm and the sun already risen. So I lay and watched the desert go past until we halted for breakfast. The side of the road was still littered with derelict vehicles of all kinds, interspersed with neat graves bearing crosses inscribed with the names and rank of German officers and men, and surmounted by their eagle-stamped steel helmets. More hastily dug and marked graves were those of

Italians, on some of which was placed or hung the ugly green-lined Italian topee. There is something impressive in the hanging steel helmet that links those dead with knights buried under their shields and weapons. But how pathetically logical and human – one of those touches of unconscious comedy which makes it difficult to be angry with them – that the Italians should have supplemented the steel cap with a ridiculous battered cut-price topee. The steel helmet is an impressive tombstone, and is its own epitaph. But the cardboard topee seemed only to say there is some junk buried here, and we may as well leave a piece of rubbish to mark the spot. Perhaps this epitaph strikes nearer the heart of those who read it.

As the day waned the road worsened, and I began to suspect more and more that the trailers of transporters were springless – as indeed they are. My pneumatic mattress flung me higher and higher in the air: as I bounced I clung desperately to its edges. The next day I transferred to the back of the towing lorry, which had springs. Whether it was Sweeney's fault or that of the R.A.S.C. officers, we had fewer and fewer halts, until there was never time for more than one cup of tea a day. The tank crews became unnecessarily bored and dirty. Yet when we did halt we wasted enough time to have had three halts a day, in moving the transporters round and round, altering their order to suit first Sweeney and then the R.A.S.C. sergeant-major. In no time Sweeney and the R.A.S.C. were hopelessly divorced from each other. Sweeney, I think, instinctively disapproved of officers who couldn't speak the King's English and were dirty in a back area, and they weren't regimental soldiers. The R.A.S.C. major naturally resented interference with his job, washing his hands of everything, and saying 'O.K., if your major wants to run it, let him. If he thinks he knows more about running a transporter convoy than we do, we don't mind.' A direct result of this was that we had to do the night guards (which, if Sweeney had let well alone, would have been found from the R.A.S.C. spare drivers).

Near Tobruk, which, to my great disappointment, we by-passed, we were met by the Colonel's party, and another stupid situation. Billy Locksley, who had just joined 'A' squadron as a newly commissioned subaltern – he had been a sergeant in 'C' squadron – had been sent with the Colonel's party, in charge of 'A' Squadron lorries. He was supposed to have gone in a jeep, but at the last moment, Andrew had claimed the jeep with a long tale about needing it as 2 i/c the road column. Tom and I were fed up because we supposed the real reason was that Andrew was one of 'the boys' – the original pre-war Yeomanry officers – and did not want the discomfort of riding on a transporter with his tank. This left us no other vehicle for Billy but the Scout car, which had been ordered to go with the tanks. The whole thing was arranged at the last moment and Billy had gone in the Scout car. The next morning Billy found that the Colonel and the other officers had arranged a mess and were eating together. They had not bothered to tell him, and being very shy, he ate his meals with the men on his vehicles. Presently Piccadilly Jim shouted for him: Billy went across and saluted. The following conversation took place:

'Good morning Billy.' 'Good morning sir.'

'Do you know' – smoothly and a little too politely – 'whose this scout car is?' 'Yes, sir. It's mine.' 'Oh, no,' said Piccadilly Jim. 'It's not yours. "A" squadron didn't send a scout car.' Billy was nonplussed, but he tried again. 'I was given orders to come in this scout car, sir.' 'Oh no you weren't,' said Piccadilly Jim. He then let loose a tirade on Billy – who had only acted on Tom's instructions – ending 'and when I give you an order, bloody well do what you're told.' No one could be more offensive than Piccadilly Jim when he tried. Billy, who as an N.C.O. had always been efficient (and not particularly imaginative), had not had much contact with Piccadilly Jim, but would have understood the reason for this arbitrary behaviour, or been mollified by it, if he had had it explained to him. He was struck by the complete injustice of it and lost his temper. He answered back. Piccadilly Jim, who, to do him justice, usually knew when he had gone too far in one of his temperamental displays, tried to make up for this by inviting Billy up to take his meals with the others. But Billy was now thoroughly sulky and refused to come. So

Tom was sent for and ordered to take Billy with him and send me. He managed to smooth things over after talking all afternoon and Billy stayed. Tom came back in a bad temper: he had slight dysentery and had wanted to rest during the halt.

At length we clattered on to the road again and began to move on, out of the desert into a green country, out of Libya into Cyrenaica, past white schools and government offices and the notices of erstwhile German and Italian parks, water-points and hospitals. Across the signpost of a hospital a board was nailed 'Under New Management'. Stencilled on the cracked plaster of outer walls and villas were bombastic Italian slogans 'W il Duce W il Re.' 'Vinceremo Duce Vinceremo' and a valedictory 'Ritorneremo'. The buildings were inviting, with cool, spacious courtyards enclosed by rooms and cloisters. We halted some twenty miles short of Barce for the night, among trees and green slopes where empty champagne and chianti bottles lay in profusion among chocolate packets and cherry tins.

On the bumpier stretches of road we had lost some of our water-cans – and unfortunately the full ones; and it looked as if we should have to forgo our tea, because there was no water-point within miles. I went up to the front of the column to see Tom about it, and as I came back again empty-handed, was met by one of my crew, who said: 'There's a Yank down the road asking for you, sir.' It was Paul Rainier, an American Field Service driver whom I had met in a dust storm on the Cairo-Alex road. That time we were stranded without a hope of getting back to camp. Sheets of rain had followed the dust storm, and we had no coats or bedding. We had slept in Paul's ambulance and he had given us some 'reel Skatch whisky' and lent me and my sergeant dry clothes and a book of which he said enthusiastically: 'You'll like *this*, Lootenant. Its varry riskay.' The whisky was a solitary bottle given him by his fiancée, to be opened only for a special occasion. We drank the half of it, and saved ourselves the consequences of being soaked and chilled.

Here was Paul again, on a return run to Barce. He said he was living on chicken and wine there, and willingly gave us all his water – twelve gallons, and all the vehicle rations from the

86

ambulance – several tins of bully. I spent the night in the ambulance again, and we drank the rest of his whisky, which he had preserved since our last meeting – my crew provided him and his friend in the next ambulance with a hot meal. We sat up fairly late in one of the ambulances over the whisky and some gin which I was able to provide. Paul came from Boston and knew the only two other Americans with whom I was acquainted. At this time the American Field Service were the only Americans we had come across in the M.E., although that morning a fleet of jeeps and lorries bearing the white star had passed us. I asked Paul who they were. 'The U.S. Army Air Corps,' he said.

Before we went to sleep, Paul gave me a glowing account of American women, who he said were the most beautiful and intelligent in the world. He invited me speciously to come to America after the war and meet hundreds of them, thousands of them. Lulled by this rosy prospect, I fell asleep. In the morning the two ambulances were on their way an hour before we moved. Paul left me a blanket to replace the one I had lost the night before, when after befriending a stray dog and giving it supper, I was foolish enough to allow it to sleep on top of the tank. The bully had not agreed with it, and being unable to jump down in the dark, it had made an irreparable mess of one blanket.

Barce is a beautiful town, its predominating colours are white, red – for roofs – and the deep green of trees. A few of the houses had CIVILIAN scrawled on them, and women and children like the peasants I had seen in Italy, carpet slippers and all, waved to us out of a welter of chickens and goats in their back gardens. They all seemed pretty happy. The town was more or less intact although a bridge on the spiral mountain road leading to it was blown, and a three-ton Chevrolet surcharged with German crosses lay upside down at the bottom of the hole. Near here, five camels had evidently wandered on to some mines on the verge of the road. An R.A.F. lorry crew were cooking their supper a few yards away across the road – the wind blowing away from them. The blackened, evil smelling corpses, almost reduced to the bones and skin, lay where they had fallen.

Before we reached Barce we had begun to be approached by

87

Senussi shepherds, who gave us Fascist salutes and wished to sell us eggs. But although 100 lire of the money taken from prisoners would buy a chicken in Barce, the desert Senussi were not interested in money. The Germans had issued them with a photographic replica of an English pound, on the back of which Arabic writing announced something. We could not read it, and two theories were put forward – either that it was to tell the natives we would redeem these for cash when we came, or that we would give them money as worthless as that paper. Whatever it said, they wanted none of our money – only sugar or tea would content them. Of these we had less than enough; but we persuaded some of them to take biscuits or bully. At first we offered them some of our own brews of tea, but they would not drink it – or if they did, made wry faces and spat it out again. They make a thick black syrup from tea and sugar, quite unlike our tea. Some of the troops defrauded them with tins of sand topped up with sugar – but they were not often simple enough to fall for that, and were never deceived by attempts to sell them dried tea leaves which had already been used.

Although we had missed seeing Tobruk, we were allowed a glimpse of Benghazi across the lake, as we skirted it. At that distance the damage to buildings was not visible – it is always astonishing to me how close you can go to a town which has been completely gutted, before it begins to look like a ruin. We saw only the Arabian beauty of white square buildings, the squat domes and the slender fingers of minarets and towers. The whole city had the appearance of a mirage.

We drove now through an avenue of dusty trees and hedges in a monotonous lazy sunlight relieved by the shadow and play of leaves: past a prisoner of war cage made by the Italians, and past the villas on the outskirts with their cool walled gardens. Soon, on either side, we saw in clusters the immense carcasses of troop-carrying planes and heavy bombers, noseless, wingless, crumpled – or surprisingly intact. Huge engines and great bombs lay about, and smaller debris.

Our destination was now declared to be El Magrum, fifty or sixty miles west of Benghazi. It seemed strange to be told that

the enemy had turned to face us again, while we waited for the
chain of supply to catch up with us: they were occupying positions lying inland from Mersa Brega – in front of Agheila, where
the road winds through impassable marshes, a narrow, easily
defendable gap. When we reached Magrum, however, we were
ordered to move on to Agedabia, and as we wound our way
along the road, on either side of which the green had given way
again to hard sand and camelthorn tufts, we were suddenly
halted and ordered to dismount where we were.

We had been ten days on the transporters, and I knew this
would be long enough for the Crusader tracks to have loosened:
I told Mudie to tighten his tracks before he slid the tank down
on to the road: he stoutly maintained it was unnecessary.
Presently I was called away by Tom and came back to find
another dispatch rider ordering my crew to lash the tank again
and go on. This would have taken too long, so I told them to
carry on as if the first order still held – several tanks of the
squadron were already on the road. I had seen Piccadilly Jim go
by a moment before and was pretty certain that these orders and
counter-orders emanated from him, in one of his 'Queen Bess'
moods, when he would fling about like a temperamental woman
and snap out so many incredible contradictions that the only
thing to do was to ignore them all and do what seemed best.
As the tank slid down on to the road I watched it come safely to
the ground, and then ran back down the line to see if I could
locate the rest of my troop. To my horror, as I was walking
back, I saw my own tank moving, turning diagonally towards a
steep incline at the edge of the road. I was just able to spring on
to the back of it as it plunged sideways into the loose sand, cutting a chunk out of the tarmac edge; but the engine drowned my
impotent shouts. One track, bearing for a moment the whole
weight of the tank, while the other churned wildly in the air,
snapped and stretched out behind the tank. It would take about
two hours to mend. I discovered that Mudie had received a
third order from a third D.R., to get off the road quickly, and,
in a not unreasonable resentment at the stream of contradictory
instructions, had driven off sideways without tightening his

tracks or getting anyone outside the tank to guide them. It was most unfortunate that it should have happened while I was away but now the harm was done. I contented myself with giving him a rocket, and told them to hurry up and mend the tank. No great harm would have been done if we could keep the incident unnoticed by Piccadilly Jim.

But Piccadilly Jim arrived two minutes later, and with one glance at the damning traces of the tank's departure from the road, turned on me the full force of an M.P.'s eloquence.

He would not allow a word of explanation but shouted in a voice audible to every driver and corporal within fifty yards. 'You are a most inefficient young officer. I couldn't be more angry with you – I would willingly kill you at this moment. Buggering up the only road we've got for the whole army. Driving your tank off the road at a totally crazy angle. If you were an N.C.O. I assure you I should break you for this – if you were a lance-corporal I should take your stripe away. Of all the bloody incompetent idiots I ever met, *you're* the worst. You can consider yourself under open arrest.' Mudie and Corporal Sandring were paying great attention to mending the track. Piccadilly Jim strode away muttering to himself in search of Tom. I had punctuated this speech with a series of 'Yes sir's' to help me keep my temper. But five minutes after he had gone I was in a blazing fury.

As we completed the move up to our area, I analysed and reanalysed the incident, trying to find some justification for this outburst. Remembering how Piccadilly Jim had first created a situation by giving three different orders in as many minutes, and then come driving down the line as though to gloat over the muddle he had created, and remembering the trouble he had deliberately made with Billy by talking at him in riddles and cursing him for something he hadn't done, I remembered a good many other little things. Piccadilly Jim seemed to be getting a sort of Agamemnon complex – I wondered if he would soon be punished for hubris. In fact, I think this was the effect which the strain of battle had upon him, which shows itself in a hundred different ways in everyone. In any case it was still true that as a colonel in action he was successful, and that he had the men's confidence.

I decided that if I accepted this rebuke tamely, Piccadilly Jim would despise me. So I wrote him a carefully and officially phrased letter, explaining what had happened, and adding that if he still held to the opinion of me he had expressed in front of my driver and gunner – that I was not fit to be a lance-corporal – I had better leave the regiment as soon as possible. Meanwhile I got another driver instead of Mudie, and sent him back out of battle. I received a letter from Piccadilly Jim by the hand of my batman:

Dear Peter

It is a great mistake ever to refer to matters which are already forgotten and done with. Napoleon* once gave this advice to a friend. Never complain. Never explain. [Is that the best you can do for a quotation?] I am liberal with my praise, of which you have had your fair share. I am equally outspoken in my criticism, and this you must, I fear, accept. In conclusion, may I recommend to you this advice which Theodore Roosevelt gave to the undergraduates of Harvard— Keep your eyes on the stars, but your feet on the ground.

I wondered how this specious treatment of awkward situations would satisfy his constituents after the war, and if he would be able to satisfy them with a couple of stock quotations. When Raoul had got into trouble once, Piccadilly Jim had used the same one (as from Napoleon) on him. As a subaltern, I had to be satisfied. In any case, the letter dispelled my pique: it amused me (and I knew it had amused Piccadilly Jim to write it). Besides, it was as near an apology as he would go.

From our new position we could see the white houses of Mersa Brega on the skyline north-west of us. In front of us lay a series of false crests, and far away, to the south-west, the long Wadi up which the Germans had advanced and beaten back the first British advance. We went out on reconnaissance in this area with two troops of the Crusader squadron. Advancing along the southern lip of the valley I came to a partially burnt-out Humber Armoured Car and beside it the grave, with a neat painted cross,

* Disraeli, anyway.

of a Royal Dragoons sergeant-major. The tinned rations in the car ration boxes were a little blackened, but made a welcome addition to our stock. A tin of treacle, which had been well heated, contained a delicious black toffee-like substance. On the northern rim of the valley, at one end of it, a standing patrol of Armoured Cars watched the Italian forward positions across the plateau to the west. The subaltern officer in charge, a boy whose red-brown, peeling face was covered with sores and slimy ointment, made us crawl up to his observation position, where he had a long telescope mounted on little tees of sand, like the telescopes through which one could look for a penny at English seaside resorts. In the dial appeared figures moving about and occasional smears of light sand where there were freshly dug positions from which the soil had not been properly cleared away.

13

Being at an hour's notice, we didn't put up our little black tent, which remained back with the 'B' vehicles. The troops of Crusaders remained hull down to anyone coming from the west, with a lookout per troop all day, and our supporting infantry manned their Vickers M.G.s on the flanks. At night we assembled to drink whisky and talk. Raoul had joined us again – and was, of course, very indignant to find Tom squadron leader. On the second evening, a pleasant, quiet chap, a captain, came to live with us, from our new R.H.A. regiment. He was to be Ken Tinker's successor, our new O.P. His name was Robin. He seemed shy and did not speak much: but Raoul drank too much and began to argue very rudely with everyone. Tom was furious with him – and so was I, for his voice had risen to a loud and hectoring monologue. He made it very difficult for me to defend him against Tom's criticisms of him. Robin had begun to answer Raoul very calmly and reasonably, and without losing his temper. We were ashamed that he should have had such a welcome on his first evening with us.

Raoul and his troop were off on patrol the next night, and we had a fairly amicable argument about snobbery. When Robin had gone, Tom said: 'He's a very good chap – but . . . I suppose it was too much to hope for another Ken.' It was plain that we couldn't expect Robin to supply Ken Tinker's quicksilver dash and brilliance in action.

At Mersa Brega began what, looking back, seems the Silly Season of the campaign, which lasted more or less as far as Tripoli. Piccadilly Jim himself seemed to be showing the strain of action in a distastrous over-confidence, an idea which grew to alarming proportions later, and in time seemed to bring the inevitable judgement of the Gods. He could not bear to sit still for long, and chafed – as we all did – while we sat and waited for orders. We had all marked on our maps the enemy positions, and those of our own troops. At last we heard that the Highlanders were going to move forward and take up a position during the night directly threatening the Italian positions. This, it was pointed out on the maps, was a clever move which would force the Italians either to retire or to fight. But in the morning, after the advance, the Italians, disconcertingly, remained there, and did not fight. Now it was rumoured that the New Zealanders, with some extra armour, were going under General Freyberg to do a 'chukker round' to the south, through marshy ground which the Germans, not unreasonably, had supposed impassable and had not even patrolled. They were to emerge on the coast at Marble Arch, and cut the enemy off. We should then go forward and fight the last battle of the North African campaign, with Rommel encircled.

Still, no orders came, and Piccadilly Jim got the Brigadier's permission to send out three troops of the Crusader squadron on a reconnaissance in force. We were, however, so restricted and cautioned that there was little point in our going at all. On no account were we to lose any tanks. A heavy squadron came somewhere in our wake. What we were to ascertain was never made clear. The Armoured Car standing patrols already knew and had reported far more about the enemy gun positions than we could possibly find out by swanning about raising clouds of dust in tanks. The Battery of twenty-five-pounders had come out behind us in the hope of getting a shoot, but if we were not to be allowed to take any risks, their shoot would be directed from extreme range.

I was ordered to draw the fire of some of these guns, while the R.H.A. O.P. tried to locate them and bring fire on them, and I took my troop out on the plateau and careered up and down raising as much dust as possible, while a few big shells bashed up the ground four or five hundred yards short of us. At last the twenty-five-pounders went into action, but apparently with no more effect than the enemy. Then the whole squadron, with a couple of infantry carriers, crept along the Wadi and moved up on to the plateau again near the enemy guns. This time their fire was too accurate to be amusing, and the two carriers were sent further forward but came scuttling back after being narrow-ly missed. The enemy were still well out of range of the tanks' guns. Robin could not get his battery into action again, although he came up and sat with us until most of the water-cans on the outside of his light American tank were holed by shell fragments. Finding that we did not move any further forward – the Brigadier was getting anxious for our safety – the enemy sent out some small trucks to drive up and down in front of his position, I suppose in the hope of luring us on. But we turned and made for home.

Guy, the second-in-command of the regiment, had been in charge of this abortive expedition. He was older than Piccadilly Jim and had been in the regiment, I think, longer than anyone. He was fantastically rich and handsome, and appeared, as indeed he was, a figure straight out of the nineteenth century. He was charming. His ideas were feudal in the best sense – he regarded everyone in the regiment as his tenants, sub-tenants, serfs, etc., and felt his responsibilities to them as a landlord. Everyone loved him and I believe pitied him a little. His slim, beautifully clad figure remained among our dirty greasy uniforms as a symbol of the regiment's former glory. He seldom, if ever, wore a beret – on this particular occasion I remember he had a flannel shirt and brown stock pinned with a gold pin, a waistcoat of some sort of yellow suede lined with sheep's wool, beautifully cut narrow trousers of fawn cavalry twill, without turn-ups, and brown suede boots. On his head was a peaked cap with a chin-strap like glass, perched at a jaunty angle. His moustache was an exact replica of those worn by heroes of the Boer war, his blue eye had a courageous twinkle, and he had the slim strong hands of a mannered horseman. He chafed at having to keep out of the enemy's range when he might have charged the guns in line, and found the matter of writing a report afterwards very tedious. When it was done, six-figure map-references and all, he showed it proudly to Tom, and said 'Glance over that will you, Tom? See if it's all in order, you know, and all that.' Checking up on the map references, Tom found the actions reported taking place somewhere in the sea off Benghazi. He pointed this out tactfully to Guy, who was quite unabashed, and said: 'Oh. Hum. Seem to have got 'em a bit wrong, eh? Where'll we put 'em?' Soon afterwards Guy was sent off on a long reconnaissance, from which no one expected to see him return, for he was not only quite fearless but reckless as well, and would not consider a recon-naissance complete until he had driven over and had a look at the enemy's faces in his jeep.

14

Whether it was the result of this display of a force of all arms or not, I don't know, but the enemy withdrew and our infantry followed them up within a day or two. We fought an action, mainly against Italian gunners, before Agheila. They fought very bravely, and the crew of one gun allowed Tom's tank to get within fifty yards of them before firing. Unfortunately for them, they missed him, only carrying away the ration boxes on one side of the tank, and he overran the gun, actually crushing one of the crew under the tank. In this action, the M.O. was badly wounded, and for a long time was in danger of losing an arm and a leg. But later we heard that he had managed to keep both, although they would never be 100 per cent useful again. His driver was killed outright. That evening, going into leaguer after dark, Raoul who had just completed his first real day in action since rejoining us (he had had little to do on the reconnaissance) had his elbow smashed by a stray shell and was taken away, back to Alexandria, out of the war, having been in action only three days and wounded twice.

The next day, we began to move across country towards the road. Those of the Italian tanks and guns which we had not destroyed or captured had withdrawn in the night. As we crawled over a rise – the Crusaders, as usual, spread out ahead – we saw the little white village of Agheila three or four miles away across a vast plain. We advanced very slowly across this plain, which was quite devoid of cover, towards the town and the high ridge of ground in front of which the coast road ran. There was no sign of movement from the tiny white squares and the green blobs of squares shielding them. Coming closer, we could make out the skeletons of aeroplanes scattered on an airfield below the town. If the gunners of the day before had been in position on that far ridge, I do not think we should ever have got across the plain. The low sun of early morning threw our shadows many yards across the ground. But there was no fire. We crawled closer, watching the skyline and the town through our binoculars. Looking to the left I saw a dark grey blur of smoke, shaped like a tree, but many times a tree's height standing up silently from the ground, like a djinn who has suddenly materialized. The djinn was about a mile away, half-left of our line of advance. As I watched, two more like him sprang up beside him, just as the first boom of a tremendous explosion reached us, the shock of its blast, even at this distance, smacking me lightly on the cheek. There was always a sensation of the miraculous, of watching a magician's trick, perhaps the Indian rope trick, when the dust of a big explosion leapt silently into the air: often its dust would blow away before the sound of it reached the ear.

We did not find out what these explosions were: there were no more of them, and we crossed the road a little west of the town, the air humming with warnings to beware of mines. But as yet no mines were discovered. They must have been plentifully sown in the ground we crossed – probably we went over some without exploding them – the water point at Agheila was afterwards found to be surrounded with them. From now on, we encountered every kind of mine, booby trap and explosive charge in the most likely and unlikely places. Some were left hidden, some exposed, some connected so as to involve anyone who set off one, in a series of explosions. They were attached to doors, furniture, loot, rubbish and on one occasion to the branch of a tree which someone idly pulled in going by. The verges of gaps in the road were mined with anti-personnel and vehicle mines, and mines were sown in the tracks of vehicles, where other vehicles might be expected to follow in hope of being safe where someone else had gone. There were explosive thermos flasks and fountain pens, presumably manufactured by those firms which in peacetime specialize in joke cigarettes which squirt ink in your face, and stinkbombs. We imagined a revision of their usual advertisement: 'Causes howls of pain. Try it on your enemies.' During the last mile of our approach to Agheila it became increasingly plain that Piccadilly Jim did not want to bypass the town without officially claiming it as our capture. Although it had already been captured by the BBC in the news the night before, this was understandable. There was a good deal of hesitation while he told first my troop, and then finally the carriers, to enter and search the town. The infantry came up on the air an hour or two later to say they had found 'some Christmas presents, pleasant and unpleasant' – booty and booby traps.

This slight hesitation behind Agheila put us behind in the order of regiments moving up the road. Another regiment caught up with the retreating guns and went into action against them without more result than the loss of four tanks and the silencing of their supporting twenty-five-pounders by counter-battery fire. We were moved up and sat on another stretch of coastal plain under fire from very heavy guns for a whole afternoon. The silly season continued. One tank could have seen as much as a whole regiment from this position, and if anyone had been killed during that interminable afternoon he would have died for no reason at all. The bursts of these shells, which luckily were lobbed over very inaccurately, were more like bomb-bursts than the explosions of shells, and at fifty yards' distance would blow in the driver's glass in the Crusader and strip the loose fittings off the outside of the tank. There was an enormous percentage of duds, one of which landed about ten yards from my tank, splattering us with mud from the rather marshy ground. It was of the calibre of the railed-off specimens in public places, and its tremendously ineffective arrival reminded me of H. M. Bateman's cartoon 'The Dud', which shows a shell with a face, expressive of gloating anticipation, flying through the air only to fall and bend its nose. It is last seen on end in the centre of a gaping crowd, oozing amatol tears, very woebegone. I moved the tank to a safe distance and went on eating biscuits and cheese and reading *National Velvet*.

15

It was during the time we spent lying about during this advance, between engagements – really from the day we first became static again at Mersa Matruh – that I began my acquaintance with most of the regimental officers and with 'A' Squadron officers in particular. From the moment when I joined the regiment in Palestine, I had recognized the unbridgeable gap between those who had been the original horsed officers, most of whom lived in or near the county from which the regiment took its name, and the 'odds and sods' who came to make up the regiment's officer strength when mechanization was complete and the un-mechanizable element safely established in odd non-regimental jobs. The faults which led to this undesirable split in the regiment lay on both sides. In Palestine 'the boys', the original Yeomen, resented mechanization, and resented the arrival of officers many of whom had served in the R.T.R. – whose feud with cavalry is a pre-war one. These new officers were not gentlemen, in the sense of *gentilhomme*. Very few of them could ride, and very few of them could afford to hunt or shoot, or knew any of the occupations or acquaintances of 'the boys'. This made it difficult for 'the boys' to find anything to talk about with the new arrivals. Being fairly lazy, they didn't talk to them at all, and continued to discuss among themselves the subject which interested them. Everyone in the cavalry in Palestine knew everyone else – so the spare time of the original officers was full and all their occupations arranged. They naturally took most of the privileges – about mechanization they not unnaturally knew nothing. The newly joined officers had mostly completed a mechanized training and knew their work reasonably well. Yet it was obvious to the cavalrymen that newly joined subalterns could not be allowed to tell the regiment what to do. If they tried to, they made themselves more and more disliked and received snub after snub. If they sat silent they had to listen on T.E.W.T.S. and training parades to senior officers talking utter nonsense in an authoritative voice. There was further the feeling among those who had seen action in Tobruk as gunners that these new officers from England had never seen action and therefore could not know more than those who had. It was a deadlock, which Piccadilly Jim's methods rather aggravated than solved. Three officers, all good officers, who would have been an asset to the regiment, asked for transfers after a month or two. One of them went, and the other two were only persuaded to stay on by a last-minute display of powerful and apologetic eloquence by Piccadilly Jim. Although I was already conscious of this atmosphere, which I had never met in my mechanized unit in England, when the battle began, I had had so little contact with any of 'the boys', except Edward, that I knew almost nothing about them. Tom alone, being in a sense one of them when he joined, was at home on either side of the barrier. The problem is, I think, unsolvable, and must simply be shelved, or will solve itself. At the beginning of the battle, when I had been a camouflage officer for eight months, they knew even less of me than I of them.

It had always been clear that Tom, within the regiment, was a careerist. He gave us, in conversations in our black tent these evenings, many accounts of his life, and I suppose the sort of self-reliance he had been forced to acquire urged him to make as much profit as he could from any situation. He told me once in Palestine that no matter how much he disliked people, his livelihood as a horse-dealer had so often depended on his tact, which he more accurately called 'a bit of the blarney', that he could get them all eating out of his hand in no time. It gave him more satisfaction to profit from people than to oppose them, which was understandable and enviable. This instinct to *deal with* people explained most of his conduct – certainly he was never sycophantic.

It wasn't long, anyway, before he had Edward 'eating out of his hand'. Edward himself was a new kind of person to me. If only he had been a little more clumsy or a little more brilliant he might have figured in Dodo or some story of Saki's. He was a man progressing imperceptibly with the inconspicuousness of English good manners, from youth to middle age. His acquaintance in England, socially, was almost complete. No title or old family name but evoked some response in him; he seemed to have attended most of the main social events of the years before the war, and illustrated papers were full of the portraits of his friends. He wrote a great many letters, and received more mail than any other three officers – indeed I never remember a delivery of mail which didn't include at least one letter for Edward. He was superficially a good listener – though very often he did not take in what was said to him – and continued to appear politely interested in anything. He could be relied on to punctuate a conversation with well-varied expressions of concern, amusement, astonishment, etc. Of anything artistic, literary or intellectual, he was most correctly ignorant – though he would often ask innocently for information to which he never listened. He never initiated a subject in conversation himself, unless conversation flagged entirely and even then he would do it by asking someone else in the company a leading question, until he had induced them to bear the brunt of the conversation again. He was a good squash player and a competent dancer in the restrained English style. His qualities were those of the perfect host, almost of a hostess. And he was the only one of 'the boys' who ever spoke to the new subalterns unnecessarily, out of pure goodwill – except Guy, who would make occasional polite inquiries of them, like a kind old squire interrogating his tenant's children over the garden gate. Edward carried modesty to the point of self-effacement, and this led to his domination

by Tom, who instinctively took advantage of it. The ban on
'shop', never more than a barely respected convention in any
wartime mess, was now quite in abeyance. In casual conversation, Tom would put forward suggestions which with his con-
versational politeness Edward accepted and afterwards found
himself committed to adopting. Tom knew as much about the
squadron administration as Edward and more than Edward
about the men, for though Edward was polite and unaffected
with the men he could not suddenly by a bonhomous, bawdy,
hearty entry into their conversation win their confidences as
Tom did. Edward was a man of one world: he never transgressed
the bounds of modesty, good manners, or good form. The only
thing I ever saw anger him was great stupidity – and that only
once in months – or breaches of good manners. Tom, whilst
winning the support of the most influential among the men, and
bombarding Edward with suggestions and improvements –
meanwhile playing Piccadilly Jim constantly on another line –
was soon the motive force and controller of the squadron's
government. He was a good officer: he looked after the men, and
his suggestions were good suggestions.

But his method soon became that of the young man who
arranges an accident so as to stage a rescue. He began to make
his opportunities instead of waiting for them. If he were sent
forward to recce a route he would report difficulties which he
had already surmounted, and a little later, explain how he was
surmounting them, over the air. I found this out when I went
with him on one of these reconnaissances, and I found that he
would pooh-pooh other people's suggestions and then, after an
interval, make them himself to the Colonel or to Edward and
take the credit for them. He never lost an opportunity, over the
wireless, of putting someone right, whether they were senior or
junior – he always did this tactfully and at the same time made
it clear that the help came from him. I suppose it was for lack of
any other mental exercise that I analysed Tom's conduct and
motives so minutely – probably I imagined a good many subtle-
ties of which he was innocent. But in a month or two he had
made such a reputation for all-round competence that Edward

and the Colonel began to regard him as a sort of universal aunt. In all this he contrived to be the reverse of sycophantic – he had more the air of coming to everyone's rescue. And in the end, if the merit of other people went unrewarded, there was no doubt that Tom earned all his rewards. He worked harder than anyone else in the regiment.

I believe all of us in the squadron saw this happening during the long series of advances and halts after Agheila. We lived with our tank crews still during the halts, but ate in the black tent, in which Edward and Tom slept. Tom was now a local unpaid captain. Each morning we walked over to the tent for breakfast, and we spent most of the day sitting in it and reading. At night we had to find our way back to our beds, lying beside our tanks, under light green bivouac sheets slung from the sides of the tank. All tanks look alike in the dark and when you have five or six hundred yards to walk it is easy to lose your direction. One night it took me nearly three hours to find my tank, and during that time I had walked right out of the regimental area and into that of the next unit but one from us. So ever afterwards I took a compass or star bearing to ensure my night's rest. Life was flat, but not entirely unpleasant. Sometimes the surface of the desert where we halted for a few hours or a few days was thick with flowers which changed the ridges and hollows whose sandy colour had for weeks been relieved only by stones, the hiding places of scorpions – or the dead grey spouts of camelthorn – into undulating distances of blue-green. The sweet scent of the flowers would come up to your nostrils even in a tank turret, moving along; it could overcome all the odours of machines.

At Christmas-time we had a 'No-Name' tobacco tin, whose label is decorative and simple, full of sweet-scented mauve flowers, something like vetches, varied with scentless dandelions and yellow, purple and pale blue dogflowers. These and the jackets of all the books we could raise between us, arranged on a table of petrol tins covered with a blanket, in a bookcase of bright plain tin – the half of a petrol tin, made the inside of the tent a true and pleasant living-room. Books and flowers are invincible beautifiers. I have often used them to make horrible

surroundings habitable. Edward received parcels at the rate of
two or three with every other batch of mail sent up to us, and
most of them contained books; the parcels I had were invariably
books, so we were not ill-supplied. In addition, we had magazines, chiefly *Punch* and *Country Life*, newspapers from England
and the Egyptian mail, the Eighth Army two-page magazine
Crusader and the Eighth Army *News Sheet*. I had one or two
German novels and magazines which I had picked up out of
enemy vehicles and positions, and a copy of *Also sprach Zara-
thrustra*, the owner of which had pencil-marked most of the
quotations in it applicable to Nazi ideas. The odd books I had
brought from division, which ranged from *Alice in Wonderland*
and a short *Survey of Surrealism* (which are easily relatable) to
the *Story of an African Farm* and the *Quest for Corvo*, were got
out and arranged in the tin whenever we halted. Edward's
favourite author was Jeffery Farnol. He liked all historical
romances, whether they were accurate accounts or utterly
improbable and incorrect – for he looked with so innocent an
eye on every world in space or time other than his own that
nothing jarred on him as occasionally it jarred even on comparatively uneducated Tom touching his equestrian knowledge,
which was timeless.

Not long after we had set up our mess in the black tent for the
last and longest of our halts, Edward suggested that I should
read to them at night, after dinner. Tom supported the request,
and I agreed because I wanted to experiment. I began by reading
parts of Sacheverell Sitwell's account of a *Court Ball in Imperial
Russia*, a fantastic embroidery of words framing or based upon
the spectacle of the waltz, the mysterious, stately, sensuous
'Valse des Fleurs' of Tchaikowsky. The descriptions of the
diversions of the Imperial city, the contrast of utter dejection,
abandonment and poverty, with riches and unrestricted entertainment and pageantry, fascinated Edward and Tom for a
little: the presentation of the regiments taking part in the march
past in the morning and the costumes to be seen in the corridors
of the palace during the Assembly for the Ball pleased them.
Meanwhile, Alastair had his own book, a volume on trout

fishing, and Billy wrote letters. Soon I saw Edward's and Tom's interest begin to flag: they had discovered there was no story to hang their attention on. How often had they both said: 'I like a good story.' Of stories they were avid and uncritical: all other literature – except, for Tom, an occasional book on Equitation or *Horse and Hound* – seemed to them to have missed its vocation.

Conversation in the tent was not particularly witty, but often interesting. A great deal of it was narrative. Tom did more talking than anyone, reminiscently, usually, about horsed days in Palestine, training and leave in the Delta, his first action at Deir el Agram, when 'dear old Ned', his friend who had been a trooper with him in the Warwickshire Yeomanry, had been killed, and Tom had won his M.C. for rescuing wounded under fire. Sweeney had got an M.C. in the same action. Tom often referred to 'dear old Ned', and would say: 'I bet old Ned's sittin' up there, laughin' like hell at it all.' This imputation to Ned of a kind of divine heartlessness never sounded very convincing.

But by far the most interesting parts of Tom's conversation were his reminiscences of his early life and of his career as a stable lad, jockey and horse dealer, with a certain amount of amateur boxing, including a Corinthian encounter, for a wager, on the grass before a village inn. His father had been a horse dealer, but had social ambitions for Tom, and educated him with the idea of his going into business. His father was the kind of man who would teach a boy to swim by throwing him overboard in deep water. His mother was devoted to him. Tom himself ran away from home and school and became a stable lad in a racing stable. After that he began to learn his technique of making himself indispensable – his stories of this epoch were revealing and explained most of his present conduct. Soon after he became a stable lad 'the old man' asked him: 'Can you plait a mane and tail, my boy?' 'I said, "No sir." "Very well, Dick, you do it for him." A week later he came to me again. "Can you plait a mane and tail, my lad?" "No, sir." And so on, for three or four times, till I tumbled to it, and when he came and asked me again "Can you plait a mane and tail, my boy?" "Yes, sir."

"H'm, about time, too" – but I had no more idea how to do it than fly. I got one of the other chaps to do mine. Then, you see, if the horse you were looking after went to a meeting, you went with it. After that I went to a lot of meetings, and I talked to the old boy whenever I got the chance, and let him tell me off and give me advice and after that he was as pleased as Punch – he used to take me with him even when I hadn't got a horse going. And then he started me riding gallops and I was in.'

Tom had progressed to riding professionally over the sticks and on the flat, and at length became a maker of horses and a dealer. He liked to recount his conversations with the famous figures of the equestrian world. His conversation overlapped at points with that of Lockett, my batman. He had married when he was twenty-one and now at thirty-one was the father of two daughters; one of whom had ridden at Olympia when she was six and was already, Tom told us proudly, bandy-legged like her father. He showed us photographs of the two children, tough-looking, snub-nosed little creatures, and his wife, a kindly looking woman with placid eyes. He himself was tall and wiry, with large ungainly hands and feet. He was a good horseman, but without elegance.

Alastair never took very much part in our conversations, although he paid great attention to them and did not give any impression of being unsociable. He was moderately tall, inclined to plumpness particularly in his face, which was highly coloured and beardless, and he had beautiful hair. He spoiled his appearance by wearing the hideous round steel, flat-lensed spectacles provided by the Army. He had not long left school, but had his own money and his being a keen fisherman probably accounted for his taciturnity.

One day when we were by ourselves in the tent, Alastair said to me: 'Don't you think that when Edward was away and Tom ran the squadron things went much more smoothly?' 'Yes,' I said. 'Why, do you think?' 'I don't know. Edward seems much too weak.' 'You mean he can be pushed into doing anything, for the sake of good manners.' 'Yes. It seemed to me Tom had much more sort of grasp of the situation. He knew his job better.'

'Yes, he does,' I said, 'and he gives the impression of being even more efficient than he really is, because he attends to everything himself. I think he does it too much – I mean, why keep a dog and bark yourself? Do you remember, when we halted at Mersa Brega, he didn't even want us to put our own tanks in position: he came round and placed each tank then.' 'Well, I thought that was rather efficient of him. Why shouldn't he?' 'The point is, he never gives any of the officers or N.C.O.s under him a chance to do anything, and as Edward or Piccadilly Jim see it from above, it looks as though no one in "A" Squadron can be trusted to do the most elementary thing except Tom, and Tom appears more and more indispensable. In fact, it's coming to the point at which no one but Tom is to be entrusted with anything, not even Edward. He's always asked to the squadron leaders' conferences. Why? No other second-in-command goes.' 'Well, I suppose Piccadilly Jim thinks he's a jolly capable chap. So he is, anyway.' 'Yes, but I resent him *trying* so hard to get in with Piccadilly Jim and get promoted before his time.' 'Oh, I don't think he does that,' said Alastair in a tone of reproach. 'I don't know. You never saw him in Palestine. He was on the job from the minute he arrived. He did things over everyone's heads, and was always charging up to Edward and Piccadilly Jim with frightfully good suggestions, and schooling Guy's horse for him, and in the other directions going down to the sergeants' mess for drinks, and having heart-to-heart talks with the men in other people's troops so that he got them to put in for transfers to his troop, and that showed everyone how popular he was.' 'You were jealous of him, I suppose.' 'Well, we resented him. There were three of us seven months senior to him – our seven months meant a lot to us, then – and fully trained. But because he was one of the Yo Yo boys and had been horsed he got in ahead of us everywhere.' 'H'm,' said Alastair, 'I suppose that was a bit annoying. But I still think Tom's a better soldier than Edward.' 'Oh, he is. He's a better soldier than you or I or Raoul, because Raoul's a bloody fool and puts everyone's back up, and you and I are too lazy to do half the work he does. He does work.' The discussion was ended by the others coming in for tea. There had been a flour issue and besides the tin mugs full of slightly salty tea, an inviting pile of jam tarts graced the table. Alastair was right, I thought, I *was* jealous, and was getting far too worked up about the whole thing. I must find something else to think about.

Billy, the fourth of my companions, had not been very talkative when he joined us. It was a bit of a jump from the sergeants' mess to the officers' mess, for a man who had spent years and years as a regular trooper, and N.C.O., learning that attitude to officers which places them in another world. He had taken a commission because his friend Harry had taken one, but Harry had been killed at Alamein before Billy even got back from his O.C.T.U., and Billy now found himself more or less lost, with Harry gone and all the landmarks of his world changed. He had been Tom's troop sergeant, but this did not mean that it was any easier to be familiar with Tom; if anything, it was harder. Edward's ability to make anyone at home quickly was never better or more gracefully displayed. He encouraged Billy to tell us stories about Harry until he lost his air of solitary gloom, and the rest of us were able to break our clumsy sympathetic silence in reply. Billy knew more even than Tom about the men: before he came to the regiment he had been a sergeant in the Eighth Hussars from which regiment most of our reservists came.

'Brown's in charge of the water cart now, isn't he?' said Edward. '*Michael* Brown,' said Billy. Reminiscent laughter from Tom. 'Why Michael?' I asked. 'Tom can tell you that,' said Billy. 'Go on, Tom.' 'Happened at Quassassin,' said Tom. 'I was duty officer, we had to sleep down in that tent where the telephone was. I was in bed one night, just getting off to sleep and hoping the bloody thing wouldn't ring, when suddenly I . . . heard . . . the . . . most monumental row, and there was old Brown outside, muckin' and blindin' to beat the band. He was canned to the wide, and I thought I'd better go and shut him up before Piccadilly Jim heard it. But I hadn't got my slacks on before little Corporal Nichols – he was doing police corporal then, poor little chap he was killed at Deir el Agram, grandest little chap you could meet – well, he'd got old Brownie by the scruff of the neck when who should come up but George

Ronson. You know, Ed, how George always said Brownie was a good boy really, and we ought to give him a stripe, all he needed was proper treatment, etc. – said to the Colonel, "You leave Brown to me, sir. I'll see you don't have any trouble with him." Anyhow, here came old George – he'd been sitting up late in the mess and I think he was in fairish order himself. He gave poor little Nichols the father and mother of a rocket – "Let go of that man at once. What the devil do you mean by manhandling him like that? Have you on a charge yourself. Leave him to me. I'll see he gets to bed." Well, Brown saw it was George and began wailin' and howlin' in the most heartbreakin' way. "Oh, Mr Ronson, it ain't my fault, sir. They never calls me by my proper name always rude nicknames, sir." Old George fell for it hook, line and muckin' sinker. "Poor old Brown. What's your first name?" "Mi-chael, sir," wails Brown. "Well, now Michael, now come along, just you come with me, and we'll see if we can get you to bed." Brownie playing up to him and saying: "You're a reel genelman, Mr Ronson. I won't let *you* down. I'll behave myself in future, I won't let it 'appen again," and off he went – old George absolutely convinced he knew how to deal with him.'

'I knew Brown in the Eighth 'Ussars,' said Billy, his eyes twinkling and the deep wrinkles beside his mouth bending to a smile. 'He was absolutely incorrigible' – Billy, like many N.C.O.s had learnt a lot of long words for the purpose of impressing squads under his charge. 'He used to boast that he was the first Eighth 'Ussar in the Citadel. He went in almost as soon as we arrived, for pinching a civvy car and smashing it up on Kasr el Nil bridge. After that, y'know, he was there as regular as clockwork. Used to have his prison set of kit. You'd go round on kit inspection – "What's that, Brown?" "Oh, them's my prison kit, Corporal." 'E used to 'ave it all folded, you know, and then sewn, so it couldn't come unfolded. S.D. tunic, pairs of socks, pants, drawers cotton long, everything, and a reel smashing bandolier. What you couldn't ever wear – it was varnished, y'see just for laying out. Then when 'e went inside, y'know, you wasn't allowed no cigarettes nor anything. Brown 'ad one of them Brasso bottles, 'e'd been down the Mousky or somewhere, and got it made with a regular top. He still had a little hole in the top, y'know, then he'd fill it with cigarettes and then screw it down and smear a little Brasso on the top – 'e was reel clever about it, y'know. Then they'd examine all his kit. And they'd find this little hole you couldn't possibly get a cigarette through, and it'd be O.K. and then Brownie'd have his Brasso and cigarettes. He used to go round when he knew he was going in and collect all the bad bandoliers and boots, and then while he was in prison he'd beeze 'em all up, reel good, y'know, like glass, and the chaps'd give him so much each when he come out.'

In this style, which suited his stories admirably, Billy told us a good deal. Between his and Tom's stories, and an occasional argument between us all, a good deal of pleasant time was passed, and books occupied the rest of our leisure.

16

Much was made by the Press of the hardships endured by the Eighth Army during this march. We often had to exist on half a gallon of water a day for washing, cooking and drinking. We had almost all our food from tins, eked out with occasional issues of flour, oatmeal, rice, or papery dried vegetables captured from the enemy. Bread we did not see for many days on end sometimes, and then only a slice or two each of the stalest, even mildewed. The water, what there was of it, tasted so strongly of disinfectant and salt that even whisky was lost in it. In some areas flies were almost unbearable – even one Egyptian fly can take up all one man's attention. They return persistently to the attack on eyes, mouth and nostrils, and are devilishly agile. Nine in every twelve men were covered with inflamed, swollen, and painful sores, on hands, faces, or legs, which took weeks or months to heal and left deep, red scars. Every man was coloured under his skin with dirt, and eyes were bloodshot with continual dust and sandstorms. But everyone shaved and washed, at least superficially, at reasonable intervals – I never went longer than two days without washing, and we all washed from head to foot once a week. Everyone had a mug of strong heavily sweetened tea – we grew quite accustomed to the flavour of the water in it, and it was always comfortably hot – three times a day. We were warmly clothed in the cold nights, and the sores and the sand were the same in camps within half an hour's run of Cairo, where flies abounded. We built comfortable latrine seats, in little houses of petrol tins filled with sand, whenever we were static for two or three days. We had papers, magazines and books throughout the journey; Cairo papers never more than two days old. Throughout the journey we were within reach of reasonably equipped and competent doctors and even dentists, albeit not so competent nor well equipped. We slept, on the whole, well; those of us who were lucky enough to fight in tanks, which do not often operate in the dark. Canteens reached us at regular intervals with a little chocolate, tobacco, beer, whisky, or gin. There was an occasional cigarette issue with rations, though these 'V' cigarettes were very bad. 'V' became the trade mark of an astonishing number of commodities in the M.E. and was always a sign of the lowest quality and cheapest goods. 'V' matches were in the proportion of about two good ones to eighteen bad ones in a packet. 'V' ink was a foul greenish-grey liquid with lumps in it.

But there were also pleasures, peculiar to the sort of life we led. It is hardly necessary to mention the immense satisfaction we derived from what comforts we did get, nor the tremendous gusto for every amenity and nourishment. And there were other pleasures which can never have the same piquancy if they are artificially introduced into ordinary existence. Each tank crew cooked for themselves, and enjoyed using their originality on the limited rations. We achieved time after time dishes of professional elegance and great variety from the invariable issues of rations. Every meal was a competition between the various tank crews. We were always a little sorry when we began to eat in the black tent again, and no longer had the right to eat the delicacies cooked by our crews, although the officers' mess cook fed us very well.

If we stopped more than two days in an area, ovens, cooking pots, fireplaces, frying pans and wash-basins were made out of cut and hammered petrol tins. Extra mugs and mess tins were made from empty tins with wire handles fitted to them. Everyone wanted to cook, and took turns in trying out new recipes. From biscuits, of which the issue varied from light and palatable ones by Peak Frean or Jacobs to dry, solid, soapy-tasting slabs made somewhere in Australia, we made porridge by smashing the biscuits to powder with a hammer, soaking them overnight and boiling the result for breakfast in the morning. When it was made with oatmeal biscuits, this was indistinguishable from real porridge. It was always warm and filling, with sugar and condensed milk added to it. From biscuits and jam, cakes and puddings were made, well browned on the outside and doughy in the middle. Sometimes there were currants to add, and a sort of duff was made. Biscuits were fried in the fat of American tinned bacon. There were immense stews of tinned meat and vegetable, Worcester sauce, onions, tinned potatoes: fried bully shreds, brown and crisp, with potato chips or crisps, and fried and flavoured rice cakes. If there were a flour issue, we had bully fritters, in batter, or fritters of dried fruit, or batter dumplings, or meat, jam, or treacle pies and pastries – we had plenty of margarine. Cheese fritters, flapjacks, pancakes, angels on horseback – the triumphs of these menus were endless. Occasionally gala feasts of eggs or sheep bought from the Senussi for tea, sugar, bully or biscuits, or on one occasion, for the two halves of an old Italian map, handed over with an air, by an Irishman. Sometimes an ill-fated gazelle or two crossed our path. Nor did we ever have the heartbreaking experience of eating good food spoiled by apathetic cooking.

For all this it was a tedious experience, the time we spent inactive in the desert, and it was a strain for someone so given to amusing himself with imaginative arrangements of the future, to be confronted with a prospect so unpredictable that I could not believe any speculation on it worth while, and so had to amuse my mind some other way. It must have been, for each man in a varying degree, a strain to have to live in the present entirely, and for months with the same companions. It was surprising how agreeable we found each other's company: we never really got on each other's nerves, and living in squadron messes, we were able to make a change by inviting people to dinner from other squadrons. These occasions, and our occasional religious services, were the only opportunities we had of seeing them: the men of another squadron were almost like the men of another regiment. I suppose we deserve a certain amount of credit for putting up with all this, but other troops have endured the desert for much longer than we did, and fought in bloodier actions. And in other parts of the world troops fought and suffered a thousand worse hardships without any credit being given them by the Press, because at the moment their exploits were neither news nor propaganda. The effort required of us was not superhuman nor unique – though for whoever organized the supplies it must have been so. Attended by their ministrations, we merely moved forward, with desultory, weeklong halts, punctuated by the occasions when we met the enemy and fought him according to our orders. I scarcely fired the gun of my tank, or read a map from Mersa Matruh to the Wadi Zem Zem, although I read a libraryful of novels. For the heavy tanks life must have been even less eventful. For whenever we moved, the Crusaders spread out in front and their crew commanders kept their eyes on the significant horizon, while they perpetually described through their microphones the prospect before them.

About two hundred miles from Tripoli we assembled and reorganized for the last lap of our advance. Piccadilly Jim gave us another of his pep talks. Perhaps it did not hearten everyone quite so much as the earlier ones. One saw a certain sameness about them, as about any effort to achieve the same effect two or three times. We were a little more encouraged by the news that we were to get brand-new tanks for this operation. Some optimists even discussed the possibility of a new type of tank, which someone was said to have seen at Base Depot – a sort of fairy-tale Crusader without any of a Crusader's defects. New pennants, and identification flags of stiff, brilliant bunting had been obtained from heaven knows where, presumably for our victorious entry into Tripoli.

The new tanks turned out to be the old tanks of another Division – a few more surprises like this, I thought, and we can begin to consider ourselves seasoned troops – for troops who are inured to the unpredictable behaviour of the various branches of the staff whose playthings they are, are inured to anything. But there were still one or two people who believed there would be a boat home for them in Tripoli harbour. The new tanks needed every kind of elementary adjustment and repair, their insides were filthy and they lacked most of the detachable bits of equipment. The men of the other Division who brought them up said they had not had time for maintenance because in their units sport took precedence over it. It is a horrible thought that this may have been true.

17

We began our approach march for the last advance on Tripoli at night, in brilliant moonlight, an interminable column of three files in which every vehicle in the Brigade was moving. These were the most physically miserable and painful hours I ever spent. The dust was like a blanket, and made breathing continually difficult, at times scarcely to be attempted. My left eye and forehead had swelled up inexplicably, the skin smarting and my head and eye aching dully, an ache as sensitive to sudden movements as an alcoholic headache. One of my eyes was covered with an eyepatch. The other had to be strained through the dust, which was a cloud before the moon and plunged us into a grey, almost complete opacity. I had one leg swollen with a big desert sore and bandaged until it looked more like a pudding than a leg. By the second night of the advance, having had very little sleep during the day, I was very sleepy. Only the bitter night cold of the beginning of January kept me awake. I had to ensure, hour after hour, that I kept my tank opposite the tank of my troop in the next file. Sometimes this was very difficult, because one file would halt and the others continue moving on. The track was marked by shaded red lights, some of which had inevitably been run over and smashed by tanks or vehicles ahead. After a few hours' sleep in the early hours of the second morning, we began our advance on Tripoli – our orders, which I had noted down on a scrap of paper in Greek characters, with a vague idea of security in my mind, gave the regiment a line of advance which ended astride the road twenty miles on the far side of Tripoli. For all our new pennons, we were not to enter the city.

Anyone who takes part in a modern battle in a tank, which is

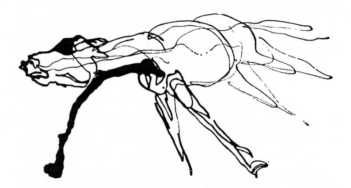

equipped with a wireless, has an advantage over the infantrymen, and over all the soldiers and generals of earlier wars. Before his mind's eye the panorama of the battle is kept, more vividly even than before the general of other times who watched his soldiers from a vantage point, or was kept posted by telephones and runners. Suppose a tank officer in the Crusader squadron of an armoured regimental group (for he is the best informed of all, more instantly and clearly aware of each event of the battle in his area even than his senior commanders). During the day or two before going into action he has listened to the scheme of orders for the whole army. He knows, or has had represented to him by a coloured diagram on a map (the main outline of which is soon fixed by the skill of habit in his mind), the position, the route, the objectives, of each Division and Brigade. In his own Brigade he knows where his own and other regiments are going, he knows where the squadrons, the supply vehicles, the guns and infantry of his regimental group are, and their radio code names. Within his squadron – let us suppose him a troop leader – he knows the positions of the other troops and of his squadron leader, and finally of the tanks of his troop. As he moves forward, the coloured lines advance across the map of his mind. He may or may not have an actual map in front of him: if he is a junior officer, it will probably be stowed, in battle. The earphones of his wireless set hang round his neck, or at noisier moments over his ears, as they are usually depicted. He hears a continuous account of the battle through these earphones. The idioms are as stereotyped as in the most ceremonial exchange of courtesies. There are things which are not said; awkward silences, epigrams, jokes: even an occasional outburst of emotion is confined by conventional phrases. The conversation follows the course of the battle with the most vivid, inimitable running commentary in the world.

The idiom of our wireless traffic, the mysterious symbolic language in some ways like that of a wildly experimental school of poets; or unemotional, dull, and thus humorous like the conversation of the two Englishmen in 'The Lady Vanishes', came from two sources. A wireless code and procedure had been laid down by someone who had vague ideas of security and no idea of the mentality of mechanized (or unmechanized) cavalrymen. For I think to a greater extent than the Royal Tank battalions, the Yeomanry found the official vocabulary unenterprising and a nuisance to learn, and supplemented it with 'veiled talk' of their own – code names and allusions as local as possible, and as typically English as possible, by which it was hoped enemy listening posts would be deceived. Unfortunately, the lack of method on the side of the speakers and the amazing deductive ability of the other side made this sort of talk quite insecure. But I can still best conjure up for myself the actual atmosphere of battle by repeating these phrases, and indeed the most officially approved wireless conversations are no more mysterious or dramatic to an ordinary listener, so that a little of this battle conversation may give a nearer impression than my adjectives and descriptions. This, then, is how the battle goes.

Each speaker has his own code name, shortened, after the initial netting calls, to a letter and a number, or simply a letter in the case of a control station. We are quite inconsistent: some of these letters change daily, some never change. Some are codes, some simply initials or Christian and nicknames (which gave us away to the enemy more often than anything else). All these disguises are used and interchanged according to whim. The enemy, who wants to find out what kind of formation we are, and if he has seen us before, and a great many smaller details, is not much deceived by our mysterious asides – but this we are not to find out until later.

Piccadilly Jim is accustomed to say – and in sanguine moments we believe him – that we have a good wireless discipline. This should mean that no one interrupts or speaks at unnecessary length, and that every vital message gets through in one. In fact, it means that we keep off the air when Piccadilly Jim is speaking, while he interrupts, dilates, or ignores messages entirely. No one ever interrupts or ignores him. For this offence, no stress of battle, except death, is an excuse. The result of this is clearly that, whatever happens, Picadilly Jim retains absolute control of the air, and, therefore, of the regimental group. It may mean that he misses important information. There are painful moments, when a somewhat facetious conversation of Jim's: 'Oh, there you are, Nuts Orange. That's just where I want you. I'm very pleased to see you. . . . Look, I'm waving to you. . . . I'm taking off my hat to you. . . . I'm blowing you a kiss . . . er . . . . Over,' and the required reply, 'Nuts Orange . . . er . . . O.K. . . . off' drown an anxious message . . . 'King 2 Ack, six enemy tanks advancing towards me on my right. They are out of my range. Could George have a go at them? Over.' But in general Piccadilly Jim is given a good idea of anything which is happening outside his own vision, by the Crusader squadron.

From the first appearance of the enemy, a Crusader troop leader, well out in front of the regiment, sees and hears the whole action, almost as if it were a pageant prepared for his entertainment: for hours on end it may continue to be exciting in quite an impersonal way. He sees a suspicious blob on the horizon; halts his squat turret almost level with a ridge and scrutinizes the blob through his glasses. Pressing the switch of his microphone, releasing it a moment to see if someone else is talking, and pressing it again, he says: 'King 2. Something that looks like a tank to my front, about three miles, I'm on your right. Over.' 'King 2. O.K. off to you. King, did you hear King 2's message?' 'King, yes. Let him keep bumming on. But be cautious. Off,' says Piccadilly Jim to Edward. 'King 1,' says Edward, calling the squadron, 'slow down a bit and have a good look from hull down before you go swanning over ridges. Over.' '2 O.K. off, 3 O.K. off, 4 O.K. off.' 'King 2, 3, 4, O.K. off to you. King 5, did you get my last message?' 'King 5. Yes. Over.' 'King 5, well bloody well wake up and acknowledge. Off.' 'Off' caps the rebuke, like a telephone receiver being hung up. We have two main sources of allusion, horses and cricket. 'Uncle Tom, what's the going like over this next bit? Can we bring the, er, unshod horses over it?' 'Uncle Tom, I'm *just* going over Beecher's myself, you want to hold 'em in a bit and go carefully, but after that it's good going for the whole field.' 'King 2 Ack,' says someone who has broken a track. 'I shall need the farrier, I've cast a shoe.' Someone else is 'having trouble with my horse's insides. Could I have the Vet?' Metaphor changes: 'King 2, someone is throwing stones. I can't see where from yet. Over,' and a little later Piccadilly Jim asks: 'King 2, now that that chap has retired to the pavilion, how many short of a full team are you?' As the action goes on, metaphors, direct speech, codes, sequences of messages are intermingled, until a good deal of concentration is needed to disentangle them. 'King 2. There are a couple of 88s on that grey ridge to my right. One is near the brew up, and the other to the left of it, about two degrees. Over.' 'King 2. O.K. off to you. Orange Pip, can you see those 88s of King 2's? Over.' 'George 4, is that a vehicle moving on your right front? Over.' 'Orange Pip, yes. Getting gunfire on now. Over.' 'George 4. Yes, I reported it just now. Over.' 'George 4, can you bring fire on to it?' 'King, have you anything to report? Over.' 'George, one of your children came up in the middle of my transmission then, when I was trying to talk to King. It's most difficult and annoying, and I won't have it. . . . Tell him to bloody well keep off the air when I'm trying to fight a battle. Off . . . er, to you. King, King, have you anything to report? Over.' 'King, King, signals. Over.' 'King 2, I think one of those guns is being towed away. Over.' 'King 2 or whoever that is, GET OFF THE BLOODY AIR when I'm trying to talk to somebody. Off. . . . King, King, signals over.' 'King, strength NINER. I'm sorry, I was talking to my jockey. Could you say again? Over.' And so on.

From the conversation it emerges that the Crusaders are held up, that the regiment on the right is under heavy and destructive fire, that there are some of our own armoured cars working forward on our left, which we mustn't fire at. The heavy tanks are engaging targets on the ridge in front of us, behind which we

can see the tops of telegraph poles. Every turn of events is recorded on the air. Someone asks for 'the little fat man' – this means they are hopelessly broken down and want the technical adjutant, known officially over the wireless as 'Tock Ack', to arrange their recovery. The regiment on our right asks for 'our bald-headed friend' on such occasions. It is these individual peculiarities which an enemy listening officer will note. The armoured cars in front, 'Our red friends on ponies, the Cherry Ps,' wheel away towards the regiment on our right – 'Uncle Gordon's boys'. Now and then an awkward, hesitating transmission creates a short silence – 'Nuts three calling. We 'ave, er, 'ad a misfortune. The horse 'as fallen, driver is no more. Can we 'ave Monkey Orange?' The gunner of a tank which has been hit, shaken by the impact of the shell, the sight of one of his friends beheaded, and another bleeding from a great wound, has forgotten his wireless procedure, if he ever knew it. If the M.O. is not already attending to someone, he will try to reach the tank in a scout car. Meanwhile, the gunner must try to get the unconscious corporal out, because the tank is burning, and bandage him roughly, because he is bleeding to death.

18

As it grew light we found ourselves advancing across a broad, flat piece of ground, towards a ridge. Near here, we knew from our information four 88s were sited, guns which destroy a Crusader with one shot at a range of a mile and a half. It was obvious that the ridge ahead had good positions for these guns, and we expected fire at any moment, as the Crusaders, strung out well ahead of the heavy tanks, crawled nearer, using every piece of scrub, mound, or fold in the floor of the plain that could give them cover from view or fire.

At length it was impossible to go any further without running the gauntlet across about five hundred yards of open ground, and the regiment slowed down to a standstill, with the Crusaders unable to sniff about any further. I asked permission to make a dash for the high ground of the ridge, as there was nothing else to do, and made for it. I was fairly sure that 88 gunners would not have let a whole regiment get as close to them as we were before firing. Already some of the big tanks behind had presented targets which they could not have resisted.

We arrived on the ridge without any excitement, all three tanks of my troop, spaced out over some three hundred yards. (I had begun the approach march of the night before with four tanks, but one had broken down during the night.) As we gained this ground we could tell from wireless traffic that the rest of 'A' Squadron had swung out to our left. We were the right-forward troop, and found ourselves on a spur running out a long way in front of us into the main wadi. To our left was a dip or valley some six hundred yards across with a table of high ground beyond, and on our right the ground stretched away on a level with us and eventually fell down into the valley again, though we could only see a false crest on our right and a false crest ahead.

My sleepiness, headache and sores were no trouble and quite unnoticeable now that I had plenty to occupy my attention. Looking across to my left front I could see a lorry towing a gun along the base of the left or southern wall of the valley. Other lorries were parked about three miles away in a patch of scrub. I could see clearly through the glasses that pieces of scrub had been attached to them as camouflage. Near where I had seen the first lorry a gully ran down, splitting the sand wall of the valley, and in this was some sort of a position with a man walking about near it.

Seeing all this activity, which was beyond the range of my guns, I had a picture in my mind of the enemy organization, which events proved to have been correct as far as it went, but very incomplete. So I reported that there was something which looked like an enemy O.P. across the valley, and asked if the infantry would send up their Vickers machine-guns, in carriers, to my position where they could fire at him, and perhaps even at the lorries, if any more of them moved. It seemed clear that we had caught some of the enemy guns in the act of taking up positions. I also asked for an artillery O.P. officer of our own attached twenty-five-pounders, who should have been up with the Crusader squadron, to come and direct his battery's fire on to the scrub where the towing and ammunition lorries of the guns appeared to be parked. But the R.H.A. attached to us were new to this role, and this was almost their first time in action with us. At Agheila they had had comparatively little difficulty as the battle there had been almost static, and they were easily arranged behind us. This time, when the R.H.A. who were with us at Alamein would have been up and into action within five minutes of my message, our new artillery were a long way behind and with them at the Battery H.Q. were both the Forward Observation Officers who should have been moving with the Crusader screen.

For two hours I went on reporting the positions of enemy guns and vehicles. One of the Shermans from 'C' Squadron, belonging to their squadron sergeant-major, was sent up on to the high ground beside me, and at last began firing under my direction. His fifth shell burst in the edge of the green patch where the enemy lorries were parked. After that, for some reason, he stopped firing and backed away down the slope.

I heard Piccadilly Jim proposing over the air to the squadron leader of 'C' Squadron that he should move forward, and took upon myself to break in with some directions of a route by which he could come without running into enemy fire. I had myself moved several hundred yards further forward among the hummocks on the top of the long spur. Meanwhile the Artillery began to fire, and their Battery Commander to call me up with inquiries as to the effect of their shots. I directed them as best I could, but without much success and in any case it would have been more practical to send up their own O.P.s, who were trained and equipped with tanks for exactly such a job, and who were still parked out of sight of the enemy. When at last I had got their shells falling into the green patch, Piccadilly Jim broke in on my observations and ordered the battery to cease fire. 'I won't have you wasting ammunition on trucks,' he said. 'When you can see a gun, let me know.' I had already reported that one gun had been towed into the green patch, and that these vehicles were the towing lorries, without which the guns could not escape, so there seemed to be no answer to this. I heard orders being given for the heavy tanks to move up. Piccadilly Jim's patience was apparently exhausted – delay was always intolerable to him.

From where my tank was lying turret down behind a ridge, I could see along a gully to my left, down into the valley on that flank of the spur, and across it to the high ground on top of which enemy vehicles occasionally appeared and disappeared. The rest of 'A' Squadron, strung out on the left, had reported them, but could not (or at any rate did not) come any further forward; so that I was now nearly a mile ahead of any tank of the regiment, except my troop sergeant. For I was now reduced to two tanks. When we had first halted in this new position, the driver glancing down at his gauges had read an alarming temperature there; a water leak had drained the whole system and the tank had to be sent out of battle. I changed into my troop corporal's tank, retaining him as gunner: he was an ambitious young man aiming at a commission, and would need all the battle experience we could give him. He stayed in the turret with me, and listened to the wireless traffic while I dismounted and went up to the crest of the ridge on foot to get a better view.

When I climbed back on to the tank I could feel its steel sides hot with the increasing heat of the noon sun. With the babble of the wireless traffic in my ears I leaned my elbows on the top of the turret and looked slowly and carefully at the panorama in front, swinging my circle of vision along the table of land away to the left, and back along the foot of the ridge to the foothills where the left-hand Crusaders lay, over my left shoulder. Then sweeping up the valley to where the green patch began and the lorries were still parked with men moving about among them. Ahead and to the right were the false crests, which prevented vision, but on our right my second tank had gone to where there was a view over into the valley.

I turned to the corporal to say something, but saw the expression of his face, looking at something behind me, change suddenly. He heaved himself quickly out of the turret, and I turned myself round, half guessing what it was. My troop sergeant was standing, in an attitude like the humble and resigned attitude of people in long queues, beside the tank. His face was covered in blood, which dripped off his chin and was splashed over the front of his battledress. Behind him one of the crew was standing, unhurt. The sergeant explained in his usual quick, assured voice. 'I went to have a look over a ridge, hull down like, and we'd not been there a second when they got us. Fifty-millimetre on the top of the turret.' The corporal made him sit down and began cleaning and dressing his wounds: the solid tungsten projectile had rebounded off the sloping side of his turret and he had received the splash of small metal fragments in his face. The tank was not damaged, he said, and while he was being attended to I ran over and verified this. The unhurt members of the crew seemed more shaken than the sergeant, who was still too dazed to be unnerved. When I got back a reaction was setting in and it seemed fairly clear that he would have to go back. I sent a call over the air for Monkey Orange, but the doctor was apparently busy already, and after half an hour I reluctantly sent him back on his own tank, reducing my troop to one.

About this time – soon after Sergeant Bayley had gone back, I looked down the gully and across the hot sand of the valley, and again saw the man moving where the left wall of the valley split. This man's behaviour and isolated position had seemed to indicate as soon as I saw him that he was a forward observation post for the guns. Seen from my new position, as from an earlier one, he presented a good target for machine-guns, which I had asked to come up to me when I was in the first position. The two carriers with the machine-guns had begun to move up near me, but had found another target on the way and had not reached me. They now arrived, unbidden, staggering along, led by the machine-gun officer in a jeep. He came across to me, a tall young man with a twinkling eye and one of those moustaches which can be seen from behind. 'Was it you who had some targets for me?' he asked.

'Yes; if you come up here, I'll show you.' We went forward, slipping a little in the deep sand, and lay down on the ridge, making ourselves comfortable and steadying our glasses. 'One across there, that little cut in the sand wall, you can see a sort of smudge.' 'Yes. Just below that black derelict on the high ground.' 'That's right. That smudge is a position. There's a chap comes out and walks about now and then. I think he's an O.P.'

'Probably is. Well, we can get on to him.' 'Then there are those lorries in the green patch. They'd be in range.' 'Not so good, because they're a frontal target. Still, we could have a go.' 'Mr Pitt, sir,' said a voice behind us. 'Captain Marco on the air, wants to speak to you, sir.' 'Sorry,' said Pitt. 'Excuse me a moment. I'm afraid he's probably going to withdraw us.' He slid down the slope and ran over to a carrier.

While he was away, I went over to my tank and spoke to Edward.

'King Five, we have George and Margaret here, in mess tins. I'm hoping to deal with the chap I spoke about, the one I think is an O.Pip across the valley. Over.' 'King Five, O.K. off.'

'Sorry,' said Charles Pitt beside the tank. 'Marcovitch says we've got to go. Wants the carriers for some other ploy. I'm awfully sorry, we could have made that chap sit up.' The carriers churned round and went away, and I had to cancel what I had just said over the air. Another half-hour of inactivity began.

I looked back down the gully up which we had crawled to our point of vantage; the walls of this gully were high enough to hide even the big tanks. I had heard Piccadilly Jim's orders for them to advance and expected to see them waddling up it at any moment. But they did not come; and I saw across the valley a solitary Sherman advancing along the flat floor of it. Two more came into view as I watched, strung out sideways and behind. They were coming slowly along under the eyes of the guns; from where I sat I could see them and the green patch where the German towing lorries were, by glancing through forty-five degrees. Shells from 88s and 50 mms., mostly high explosive from 88s, had been bursting fairly near my position all day, but I did not think they had seen any actual targets most of the time. Sergeant Bayley's showing himself, however, had had such an instantaneous and destructive result as showed that the enemy gunners could be accurate at the least opportunity given them. And now three large tanks were moving slowly up an open valley. Not as much as 4,000 yards lay between them and the enemy. I had no time to repeat my earlier reports and warnings before a shower of light and dark grey-blue smoke suddenly and silently flew from the side of the leading Sherman's turret, like the goddess Sin springing from the left shoulder of Satan. The tank was in flames before the noise of impact and explosion reached me. I saw two figures struggling at the top of the turret, heaving at a third as limp as an effigy. As they staggered clear with their burden, I saw the other two tanks reversing; and turning at a new noise, found the carriers, four of them with riflemen and bren guns, returning up my gully. With them came Captain Marco, the motor company commander, beetroot-faced like a stage farmer, in a White Scout car. He was known to my regiment as the man from the Mousky, since his origins were non-Aryan and obscure, and he had been born in Cairo. The Mousky region of bazaars and alluring scent shops, where all origins are lost, had been suggested by some wit as the quarter of the city where Marco began.

He came up to me and said, 'I'm sending Willy Root here' – an unfortunate subaltern – 'out with the carriers to see what he can see. What's the form up here?' 'Well,' I said. 'He can see as

Men killed by aerial attack.

much from here as he'll see from anywhere. There are no more gullies forward of here, and he'll get shot at very accurately as soon as he moves out of this gully. I'll show you what I can from here.' And I pointed out the same split in the sand wall, the green patch, the clefts where guns might be, and as a cautionary measure, the burning Sherman and its column of black smoke. Mousky didn't answer me, but said to Root: 'You see what this officer says?' (Root had just been commissioned and Mousky still spoke to him as he had been used to when Root was a sergeant.) 'Now take your carriers across there – you won't get shot at, they're not tanks, and bring back some information.' This order meant nothing. It was clear that the low, exposed ground of the valley would afford no view not available from our cover, and 'bring back some information' was a very nebulous mission for four carriers full of armed men in broad daylight. I could say nothing: Mousky went back down the gully in his car, and the four carriers moved out into the open valley. I swung my glasses towards the enemy positions. They would be firing any moment now, and I kept my eyes skinned for a flash. I looked backwards and forwards over the suspicious ground for perhaps five minutes, but saw nothing. Then I heard the carriers bucketing and creaking back into the gully. Three of them. The fourth was blazing some two hundred yards nearer to the enemy than the destroyed tank.

From my position I could report no more than I had already reported. But this information had clearly made no impression, and three men at least had been killed in the last hour on ground which I had tried to warn them off, and of which even their memories of schoolboy adventure stories should have made them wary. There was no more cover to permit my advancing any further, but it seemed that I *must*, somehow, find some more definite and arresting news of the enemy guns. I looked at the valley and saw a shallow groove in it beginning near the wrecked carrier, but beyond it, and running up the valley. This groove might barely hide my tank or most of it, if I could get there across about 300 yards of open ground. It would take too long to work round behind the smoke of the burning tank; I wanted speed, and could only achieve it by going straight. A straight path would take me behind the much slighter smoke-screen rising and slanting from the carrier, and between the two burning vehicles.

I explained to the driver what I was going to do, and told him to back the tank, so that we could get the longest possible run under cover, and get up as high a speed as we could before coming into the open. We started grinding away in first gear and got into top about thirty yards clear of the last cover. I was relieved when we arrived in the low ground without being fired at, and we began to move up the groove, finding that the wall of it rose on our left and lowered on our right, until the cleft ended in a little ridge of sand to our front, about 400 yards nearer the enemy. We were covered ahead and to our left; glancing to the right I saw a sort of cover provided by the spur which we had left, and which ended parallel with our new position. The side of the spur was about a hundred yards away to our right. Near the end of the spur was an erection of sandbags built into the side of the slope, evidently one of the last positions vacated by the retreating enemy. I saw there was a wireless aerial standing up from it, and thought, 'They don't usually leave wireless sets behind,' and then, 'Perhaps there's someone in it.' A man's head and shoulders emerged from it as I looked, and as he put out his head he pushed up two flaps, groped inside for field-glasses, adjusted them, and began to look carefully at something in front of him. To see me, he had only to turn his head to the right. When I saw the flaps lifted I realized it was the turret of a heavy tank; sandbags had been hung on the sides of it, as they often were in front, to give extra protection. This tank's gun would send a solid shot through my turret and out the other side at twenty hundred, and he was not a hundred and fifty yards away.

The great thing, said my mind, is not to flap. I involuntarily said, 'Take your time' aloud about twice, and touched the Corporal, who was still peering through his glasses at the green patch. 'That chap is a Jerry in a Mk III,' I said. 'I should quite like to shoot him up before he sees us. Don't hurry, but make sure you get him first shot.' As he swung the turret round, and the German observer continued scanning the ground away behind us, I said over the air: 'King Five, I'm afraid I've bummed on a bit too far, and I'm about a hundred yards from a Jerry tank. He hasn't seen me yet, and I'm going to try and crack him before he does. Over.' My stomach was turning over inside me. 'King Five,' Piccadilly Jim answered before Edward could acknowledge my message. 'Give the bugger hell,' with a kind of refined emphasis quite divorced from the words. This is a long description of a few short minutes, but the various incidents of that short time did not seem to arrive with less unhurried deliberation than is needed to describe them. I saw, did, and said all these things, and thought many irrelevancies – there was too, a kind of physical shrinking-in of my belly, opposite which the armour plate might at any moment admit a projectile. As the turret swung I watched the heavy barrel moving and said, 'On. Fire when you like, but hurry up.' There was a long moment of silence. I remembered suddenly, this Corporal is an operator not a gunner. 'It's stuck,' the Corporal said, in a voice as if he could not get his breath. He looked up at me, and I thought, 'I don't know if I'm flapping, but he is.' 'What's the matter?' I said, with agonized patience. 'It's stuck, it's stuck. It won't elevate.' The Corporal began to heave and wrench blindly, like a man who has lost his temper. His fingers fluttered to the safety catch, flicking it on and off. That was conclusive. I said into the microphone: 'Driver advance. Driver right. Speed up, speed up,' and switching to the A set: 'King Five, my piece of ordnance has let me down. I'm getting out. Over.' 'Bad luck,' said Piccadilly Jim's voice. 'I'm very sorry.' I looked up. We were heading directly towards the German, now only fifty yards or so away. I had already heard the report of one shot, and now cried: 'Driver right, RIGHT' into the mouthpiece. He continued steadily forward; I realized I was still switched to A set, shouting my agonized instructions to the whole regiment, but inaudible to the driver. I switched hastily and repeated, 'Right, Right,' until he obeyed and swung round. 'Speed-up or you'll be blown to glory,' for he was grinding along in second gear. I looked at the enemy again but he had slid behind the ridge out of sight. He must have thought we were going to ram him. I was sweating and out of breath.

Piccadilly Jim now engaged in a long conversation and I did my best to tell him exactly where I had just been, while I turned cautiously along the foot of the spur. Through the intercommunication the driver apologized for being unable to speed up: only first, second and reverse gears would engage – my last remaining tank was dying on my hands. As we crept forward, I heard Ken Giles, a subaltern in 'B' Squadron, reporting the position of what appeared to be my late adversary. 'I am engaging him,' he said, and I heard the noise of his '75' somewhere not far behind, among the mounds of the spur. His voice recalled to me a description he once gave us at dinner of fighting a battle in a Grant tank: 'The "75" is firing. The "37" is firing, but it's traversed round the wrong way. The Browning is jammed. I am saying "Driver advance" on the A set, and the driver who can't hear me, is reversing. And as I look over the top of the turret and see twelve enemy tanks fifty yards away, someone hands me a cheese sandwich.' At the moment this seemed just another true word spoken in jest.

Coming up the slopes of the spur, I told the driver to be ready to halt instantly on my order. I soon saw what I was looking for – a straight edge outlined against the sky, and said, 'Halt. Now slide down a yard or two. O.K.' By standing on tiptoe on my turret, I could just see the extreme edge of my target. By reversing or advancing a few yards either way, I lined the tank up on it, so that the six-pounder, without traversing at all, pointed on the correct line. I said to the Corporal: 'Sure you'll be able to fire this time? You've only got to pull the trigger.' I made him stand upon the turret so that he could see the metal edge of the target. Then we got down in the turret and began to move forward. But remembering previous experience, I gave a precautionary look to the right as we climbed higher. What I saw stupefied me again.

Mousky, in his scout car, was moving parallel with us, on the top of the spur. I saw him first, trembled for him and pointed

towards our target, realizing in the same moment that he could
see it better than I, and that it could not be what I had thought.
We climbed fully atop of the spur and I saw, first that our
objective was not a tank, but a 50-mm. gun, which had evidently
been hastily abandoned, and then that beyond Mousky a whole
squadron of Shermans, 'C' Squadron, was advancing majesti-
cally in line along the top of the spur. I was dumbfounded – a
moment ago, it seemed, I had been as much as a mile ahead of
the regiment, and now the regiment had caught me up and was
passing me in such a leisurely continual progress as suggested
that all enemy resistance was at an end. What was more disconcerting was that there could now be no Crusader screen
ahead of the big tanks, who were not accustomed to move
across country without one. I knew the remainder of 'A'
Squadron, away on the left, could not have moved across
without my seeing them. I could only decide that some momen-
tous change had come over the situation as I was scuttling back
from my tête-à-tête with the enemy. I moved with this general
stream of traffic into a large bowl-shaped depression behind a
semicircular ridge which was the end of the spur. Beyond this
ridge the open valley ran without a suspicion of cover to the
enemy positions across the wadi, perhaps two miles away.

I climbed on to one edge of the bowl and saw a German tank
heading away across the valley in a cloud of dust: this seemed to
be the tank I had been stalking. I reported to Edward. 'The
gentleman I met just now is heading for home, flat out.' Edward
did not acknowledge the message, but Piccadilly Jim who must
have been behind and out of sight, for the spur was honey-
combed with false crests, said exultantly to 'C' Squadron,
'X-ray, you've got them on the run. Keep after them.' At this
moment my tank's engine failed altogether. We were down on
the floor of the bowl, unable to observe. This was the worst
thing that could have happened. If I could have looked over the
top at this crucial minute, I might have been able to correct
Piccadilly Jim's (and my own) impression, evidently strengthened
by my last message, that the enemy were on the run. But before
we could make the tank move again, a Grant mounted the tip

of the bowl and was instantly hit and set on fire. I tried to report
this, but was reprimanded by Piccadilly Jim for bad security.
He continued to urge the heavy tanks forward: the whole of
'C' Squadron assembled in the bowl. With them came – far
too late – the Honey tank of the R.H.A. Observation officer. The
Corporal had meanwhile dismounted and was giving first aid to
some of the crew of the burning Grant, who were crouching in a
hole dug near a half-tracked vehicle, evidently the towing
vehicle of the abandoned gun. This tractor had been set alight,
but had not caught fire properly and was now sending up only a
thin curtain of smoke. I asked Edward to send someone over to
join me, and heard him order somebody across.

Enemy guns of all sizes now began to shell the interior of the
bowl. The Corporal came running back and we moved across to
the other side of the bowl, where the shelling was slightly less. It
was soon clear that the enemy had the range to this depression
accurately measured, and I saw there were stone cairns on the
edge of it which must have been built as aiming marks. I saw a
Crusader moving along the outer edge of the bowl on the skyline:
it was like seeing an inexperienced person walking a tightrope.
There was only one man in the Squadron who would be stupid
enough to move along a skyline when he could see shells arriving near him, and that one tank was already on fire in his way.
This was a new subaltern who had joined the regiment as a
reinforcement from Base depot. He had been sent to 'C'
Squadron, who after living with him for a week had palmed him
off on to 'A' Squadron to replace Raoul. He had not been in
action with us before, but had already an odd reputation because
of his habit of saluting everybody, even the subalterns of his
own Squadron, several times a day. The providence of fools and
drunken men seemed to be guarding him at the moment, for he
moved down off the ridge at last, and seeing another Crusader,
came towards us and halted about ten yards away, making a
motion of saluting with his hand.

We sat there with heavy tanks and shellbursts all round us, not
feeling comfortable. Once I moved up and looked over the edge,
but what I saw only confused me. A Sherman was moving

sedately across our front along the valley, unmolested and all alone. Near it were some three-ton lorries of British design, apparently parked. But the fire continued. Twenty-five yards away John Simpson's Sherman, still distinguishable by the black eye of Horus on its flank, was suddenly enveloped in black smoke and flame. I ran across as the crew came tumbling out with a Pyrene extinguisher. John was already using his when I got there. An oil shell had hit the front of the tank, and our extinguishers made very little impression on it. We began to cut the kit away from the kit rail, sawing at it with the blunt-bladed knives, like huge rusty fish slices, provided for hacking scrub as fuel. But before we had got two packs off, the driver who was still in the tank, released the brakes and it slid backwards towards the bottom of the bowl. The larger mass of the conflagration remained blazing on the sand. The rubber track and a patch of incendiary liquid on the front of the tank were still burning, but the track extinguished itself in turning, and we had soon put out the rest. 'Thanking you,' said John, climbing into his turret again. I ran back and remounted my own tank. As I picked up the earphones I heard Edward say: 'King Five, King Five, are you O.K.? Over.' 'King Five, yes,' I said. 'But I can't see much; we're under fairly heavy fire. There seem to be guns all round this place. I'm trying to find a place where I can see without being potted at. Over.' 'King Five, have a look towards the sun. Off.' The sun was now on our left, and the tank starting forward, I could see a Grant which seemed to be observing safely near the half-tracked derelict, and decided to move up near it.

As we passed behind the Grant, labouring in second gear, a 50-mm. shot came through the side of our turret with an immense clang. The tank stopped and rolled back a few yards. My first sensation was that the whole turret had collapsed inwards on us and was pinning us in. I couldn't open my eyes, the right side of my face seemed to be very sore, and there was a small pain in my left leg. I heard the Corporal say: 'Get out, sir, we've been hit' as though from a long way off, and simultaneously I was able to move, as if his voice had broken a spell.

I climbed out on to the back of the tank, with the earphones still on and the microphone dangling on my chest. I was able to open my eyes for a second but they closed themselves and tears poured out from under the lids. I realized the wireless was still working,

Sam & Crew.

and said: 'King Five, my horse has copped it. Wireless O.K., but we shan't be able to take any further part in the show. I'll just have a look at the damage and tell you the extent.' 'King Five, that's the second time. You *must not* say such things over the air,' said Piccadilly Jim. I could not see what harm it could do if I had said clearly, 'My tank has been hit,' since the enemy must have observed the hit, but supposing my reasoning must not be working properly, said: 'King Five, sorry. I'm a bit dizzy. Over,' and Piccadilly Jim replied, characteristically: 'King Five, I'm sorry you're dizzy. But you really must not say these things. Now take care of yourself. Off.'

I now had my eyes open and could see that the Grant beside us was burning beautifully. It must have been hit a few seconds after us. The faces of its crew and of my own corporal watched me from a German vehicle pit a few yards away. I climbed off the tank and with the idea of saving my kit from the risk of catching fire, hauled my valise and pack into the pit. I said to

133

the Corporal: 'Where's the driver?' 'He must be in there still, sir.' I went and peered in at the driver's window in the front of the Crusader, which was not closed down. Inside, Dunn, the driver, lay with his eyes closed, his face chalky and his mouth open, showing a few yellow teeth and a lolling tongue. Like Old Man Mose, he didn't make a single move and I thought he was dead, but as I was turning away his eyes opened and he said almost in a whisper, 'My neck, my neck.' I called two of the others out of the pit and we were able to get him out, although I'm afraid we hurt him a lot doing it. We lowered him in to the pit, where he complained of intolerable pain. I remembered that the officers had all been given individual morphia syringes, containing one dose, before the battle, and searched my pockets vainly for mine. I looked round and saw that Black was still where he had stopped when we were hit, some ten yards from the blazing Grant, and gazing vacantly at the edge of the bowl about ten yards in front of him. I thought, doesn't the bloody fool know it'll blow up in a minute, and went across to him. He did not see me. I stood beside his tank and shouted at him, but he had his earphones on, and continued to stare stolidly ahead, like a cow. 'Give me your morphia,' I shouted. The Grant beside us blew up with a great roar, twelve yards away. The twenty-four tons of metal disintegrated; the turret flying one way, the sides and suspension wheels another, left a mass of burning wreckage, and one of the great rubber tracks uncoiled like a dead snake. By some chance I was hit by someone's bedding and found myself hurled against the side of the Crusader, wrapped from head to foot in blankets. I glared up at Black like a Red Indian; and he stared down at me with a wondering eye. He was evidently trying to decide why I was dressed in blankets. I shouted again, 'Give me your *morphia syringe.*' He took off his earphones and after shouting only once more, I saw him fumbling inside the turret. He handed it out to me. 'Now go away before you're hit,' I said. I went back to the pit.

The Corporal injected the morphia into Dunn's arm: the needle was very blunt and a good deal of the stuff flowed out of a crack at the base of the needle and dribbled on the skin. Dunn did not seem any better for the injection. This was not surprising since it later turned out that we had been given by mistake a preparation for waking up people under anaesthetic.

The shells continued falling, and no one was much inclined to stir out of the pit. But the engine of my Crusader was still running: the shot had made a clean round hole in the underside of the turret, and must have passed within a few inches of my stomach and smashed against the base of the six-pounder. I had had a look at the damage during the business of getting Dunn out, and now that he was as settled as possible I felt I ought to move the tank out of the area of shell fire. When I stood up to go and do this the Corporal said there were half a dozen packets of Players on top of the wireless set, and would I please bring them back with me. I got the Players first and then climbed out of the top of the tank and in again through the front. I settled myself in the driver's compartment, revved the engine, and engaged first gear. I let up the clutch as slowly as possible and the tank began to grind forward. When I had gathered speed I engaged second gear but the engine sputtered, coughed, and stalled. I tried to restart it in vain. So I pulled myself up and out again, dropping off the bows of the tank on to the ground. The shell-fire seemed to have slackened in our neighbourhood and I looked round the area. On the edge of the bowl, about fifty yards away, was a German tank.

It must have arrived after I had stopped moving, for the commander of it was gazing over my head at the ridges far behind me. I dodged down and looked hastily round. Until this moment I had felt comforted by the presence all round our pit of the 'C' Squadron Shermans. In the back of my mind I had supposed someone would soon arrive to pick us out of our hole. My last glimpse of the enemy had been of a tank escaping hurriedly westwards, and I had had no doubt in my mind that the nearest Germans were a mile or two across the valley. For one tank to advance again against a squadron would be madness. But I saw now that although all the Shermans were still there, those reassuring shapes which I had seen out of the corner of my eye while I was extricating Dunn, injecting morphia, bandaging –

there was not a living man in any of them. They were dead tanks, burning, smouldering or silent and useless. This was the biggest shock.

'Capture,' I thought suddenly. 'I shall be captured.' There was no sign of the regiment. Only the shells of tanks, and the enemy, coolly surveying the landscape. If I ran to the hole they would find us all. I think I was as near panic as I have ever been. My thoughts flickered with my glance over all possible refuges. I began to run, keeping my tank between me and the enemy: I was bound to come into the open and to make an easy mark for their machine-gun, and I thought of this and accepted the thought. I did not care if they shot me but I was unnerved by the thought of capture. I ran about two hundred yards. After that the headache of the early morning reasserted itself, the sore in my leg throbbed insistently under its dirty bandages, the scorched places on my face and the scratches on my leg made themselves felt, and I had no more breath to run; I was quite exhausted. I began walking, too tired to care any more about escape, until I should have a breathing space.

I walked forward blindly and almost tripped over a man on the ground. He was a 'C' Squadron corporal, and his right foot was not there: the leg ended in a sort of tattered brush of bone and flesh. He said something which I could not hear, or which my mind would not grasp. After he had said it twice, I realized he was asking me not to leave him behind. To carry him seemed to my tired muscles and lungs impossible. I looked ahead and saw the sandhills stretching for an eternity, without a sign of life. 'Kneel down,' he said. 'I can get on your back.' I got on my knees and he fastened a grip on me like the old man of the sea. I tried to stand up, and at last achieved it, swaying and sweating, with the man on my back; his good leg and his stump tucked under my arms, his hands locked at my throat.

'Don't grip my throat so hard if you can help it,' I said. He relaxed his hold at once, and slid his hands down to my chest. I began to walk forward, with little idea of what I was going to do. As far as I could see I had half to three-quarters of a mile to go under the eye of the German tank commander, before I could cross a ridge and get out of his sight. No shot was fired, while I walked about fifty yards. Then an officer and two men of 'C' Squadron came out of a square pit where they were sheltering and helped me in with my burden, which we lowered carefully. Bill, the officer, had not long rejoined the regiment from a special job. He and the others began to put a shell dressing on the wounded man's leg, while I sat panting and regaining my breath. I realized I was still clutching two or three packets of Players which I had taken from my tank, so I handed them round. I told Bill about the German tank: I was still obsessed with the idea of escaping capture. I think if it had been hailing machine-gun bullets I would have stepped out into them without caring. My mind was not working properly. 'If we all stay here,' I said to Bill, 'we shall probably be captured. I think someone ought to go back and try to get a vehicle to get us out.' This was quite a sensible suggestion, but a wish was father to it. Bill agreed and said: 'You go. These are my chaps, so I'll stay. Corporal Hicks, Dumeny, Cairns, you go back.' We stood up and left the pit. A machine-gun somewhere opened up; I heard the noise of it, but did not see any sign that the shots were aimed at us. The men with me were walking along bent double as though searching the ground. I said to them: 'It's no good ducking down. If you're going to be hit you'll be hit. Run across the open ground. Run.' They began to trot reluctantly, and I ran ahead. Presently I saw two men crawling on the ground, wriggling forward very slowly in a kind of embrace.

As I came up to them I recognized one of them as Robin, the R.H.A. Observation Officer whose aid I had been asking earlier in the day: I recognized first his fleece-lined suede waistcoat and polished brass shoulder titles and then his face, strained and tired with pain. His left foot was smashed to pulp, mingled with the remainder of a boot. But as I spoke to Robin saying, 'Have you got a tourniquet, Robin?' and he answered apologetically: 'I'm afraid I haven't, Peter,' I looked at the second man. Only his clothes distinguished him as a human being, and they were badly charred. His face had gone: in place of it was a huge yellow vegetable. The eyes blinked in it, eyes without lashes, and a grotesque huge mouth dribbled and moaned like a child exhausted with crying.

Robin's mangled leg was not bleeding: a paste of blood and sand, or congealed slabs of blood, covered it. I thought it would be better left as it was than bandaged, now that the air had closed it. 'I'll go on back,' I said, 'and get hold of something to pick you up, a scout car or something. Stay here.' I ran on. Before I had gone a hundred yards I was ashamed: my own mind accused me of running to escape, rather than running for help. But I hurried on, determined to silence these accusations by getting a vehicle of some kind and bringing it back, in the face of the enemy if necessary. I knew that if only I could gain the cover of the ridge and stop to think, and if I could find where the regiment had gone, I should be able to reorganize myself and go back, as I had after the first encounter with the tank.

Round a ridge of sand beside me the new lieutenant came walking. He raised a hand in salute and began to talk in a foolish flow of words about how his tank had been hit in the engine and why it had happened and how it would never have happened if only he had done such and such a thing, *und so weiter*. I walked beside him. I said: 'We must find the chaps, and get something to get the people out of those holes, and tell Piccadilly Jim how

Arab dogs

close the enemy are.' I was searching the ground ahead with my eyes, my companion looking at the ground by his feet. We almost walked past the remains of the regiment, drawn up on our left behind a ridge, because I was looking for them ahead and he was not looking at all. The nearest vehicle was Mousky's scout car, which I had had in mind, and I ran across towards it. In it sat Mousky and his driver. Another infantryman stood beside it. As we came closer I could see it was buried over its differential in sand, and would take anything up to an hour to shift. No one had yet begun to try. But beyond it was the scout car belonging to the Technical adjutant, Bert Pyeman, an ex-regular N.C.O., contemporary of Mac's. Bert was driving away from me. I shouted at him, but two of the Shermans fired simultaneously and my voice was drowned. Before I could shout again, my companion said: 'Look out. There's a trip wire.' I knew already; I had just tripped it. I should have thrown myself down at once, but a sort of resignation prevented me, and I walked on a few steps before the mine exploded.

I remained standing, numbed. It seemed impossible that any-thing could hit so hard and leave me on my feet: and as feeling came back, I shrank from movement. But the explosion of a second mine suggested to me that I ought to throw myself down, and I toppled forward and sprawled on the sand. A third mine went off, further away. I was aware of the new subaltern lying on the other side of the trip wire, which stretched between us as taut as ever. It was a bright new wire strung through wooden pegs: I realized that I had seen it and discounted it because of its newness, and because subconsciously I had come to expect such things to be cunningly hidden. People ran towards us from Mousky's scout car. I shouted to them: 'Look out for mines. Don't explode any more.' One of them said mistakenly as he came up, '*You're* all right, sir,' in a soothing sort of voice. I found I could raise one arm and waved it at Bert Pyeman whose attention the bang had attracted. He swung his little beetle of a car round and came across to us. 'Don't try to get up, Peter,' he said. I couldn't even try now: and it seemed incredible that a minute or two ago I had shouted out, for now I could only raise

a whisper, in which I said: 'Can you get me out of here?' somewhat unnecessarily. 'O.K. old boy, we'll get you out. Can you
heave yourself on to the back of the Dingo if we support you?'
Bert had finished putting a very tight bandage on my right foot,
which had been bleeding a lot. 'Yes, I think so,' I said.

19

Bert and Mousky helped me on to the back of the scout car.
Two others were hoisting Black, who was moaning and crying
out: 'Look out for my leg. I must have my feet higher than my
head or I shall bleed to death. Look out. *Look out*. Oh,' as they
put him beside me. I said to Mousky: 'Is that whisky I smell?'
He admitted it was, but did not offer me any, so I said: 'Can I
have some?' and he handed it over with some reluctance. It was
Johnny Walker, and I took several swallows from the bottle
gratefully. I had a little more voice to return thanks with. Black
pushed the bottle away as if it were red-hot and said: 'No – no.
Take it away,' petulantly. His pain and shock had had the effect
of making him bad-tempered. I could hear Edward's voice
coming out of the earphones on the seat of the scout car, but I
couldn't reach the microphone to answer. I asked Bert to answer
it, to tell the Colonel the positions of the enemy and to arrange
about rescuing Alan and Bill and all the other wounded. Thinking that later I might not be able to tell him, I said where they
were in detail. He answered me in a sort of bedside reassuring
voice, and did nothing about answering the broadcast appeals for
Black and myself. This was not surprising because we were still
under fire, and Bert was trying to guide the scout car over
hummocks and through possible scattered mines as gently, yet as
quickly as possible, and to hold Black on the back, who was in
danger of slipping off. The pain in my foot, which Bert had tied
up very tightly to stop it bleeding, was increasing. I said to
Bert: 'Don't take any notice if I moan. I like moaning,' and with
this excuse began to moan in a jerky way, dependent on the
bumps. It was a way of taking my mind off the foot. The rest of
me was very sore but nothing unbearable. Black, unfortunately,

approved the idea of moaning and began to do so verbally, crying out: 'Stop. Stop. I can't go on.' I gave up my own moaning and joined Bert in saying: 'Only another two hundred yards' – although I could see if I turned my head, that we were nowhere near the R.A.P. yet, and had probably another 800 yards to go. I thought at the time that Black was making far too much fuss. But I found afterwards that he wasn't making nearly enough. He had been hit in the face, arms, hands, stomach and legs, and when I saw him later, after eight months in hospital, he was still unable to see clearly out of one eye, which was drooping in his face, and could not work his hands properly.

Once we stopped near a three-ton ammunition lorry of another regiment, whose crew were brewing tea, and I was handed a cup of it, from which I took a few wary sips for it was very hot. Black refused to take any, and resumed his monotonous chant of 'Oh . . . oh . . . I can't go on.' At last we arrived at the Regimental ambulance where I slid off the scout car and lowered myself on to a stretcher, with help from two 'B' echelon drivers who had come up to the ambulance as we arrived. I felt cold, and was given a blanket. While the M.O. examined Black someone gave me a fresh cup of tea, which I drank in gulps. I don't like tea, but that moment I would have exchanged it for nothing else. Hart, an American trooper in 'A' Squadron, who was now the driver of the M.O.'s scout car and was later to lose a leg at Mareth, stood and talked to me. He gave me a cigarette, bending his tall body down to light it, and continuing to talk easily in his lazy voice.

Presently the M.O., his red face covered with taut, weather-beaten skin, came and grinned at me; his mild eyes smiling above a mouthful of horse's teeth. 'Let's have a look at you,' he said. 'Wait a bit,' I said hastily. 'I'll take off my shoes and my battle-dress top.' My trousers were already hanging in ribbons. But he insisted I must lie still, cut off my suede shoes, my new N.Z. battledress blouse, bought only a week before at a travelling officers' shop in the Sirte area, and my suede leather waistcoat, which was quite irreplaceable. He did not cut the seams of the garments, nor the laces of the shoes, but destroyed everything with haphazard cuts of a huge Strewelpeter pair of scissors. When he had got the clothing off me, I found that apart from two small scratches made by the A.P. round which had hit my tank, I had a hole in my right foot, made by something still lodged inside it; there were other bits of metal or wounds in the calf of my right leg, in my left thigh, and in the small of my back; under my left arm and in my left shoulder. I still had a bandage covering my left leg from knee to ankle over a large open sore; and the mysterious swelling over my eye had now burst, which the doctor decided to call shingles, putting a patch over it. The hair, eyebrow and moustache on the right side of my face were scorched away, and I was smeared with some sort of ointment. Almost covered with dressings from head to foot and still wearing the filthy remnants of my clothes, I looked vainly round for someone from the Army Film and Photographic Unit. After my whisky and hot tea I felt thoroughly cheerful and ready to produce a traditional grin to go with my costume. I could readily forgive the destruction of my clothes to achieve such an artistic whole as my appearance after treatment. And the few hundred yards we had come bumping on the scout car were the first few hundred yards to Cairo, Alexandria, the Delta and the delights of civilization. I lay back and considered with utter selfishness how I would be washed and rested and fed in hospital, and what I would do, who I would see, on my sick leave.

These pleasing thoughts were soon spoilt by doubts. Perhaps I should get no further than Tobruk: I wasn't badly wounded. And I seemed to remember hearing that sick leave was no longer granted, except in convalescent depots, where it was not worth having. But at length an ambulance from the forward dressing station arrived and Black and I, followed by voices of farewell and good wishes, set off on the first lap of our course of over a thousand miles, to the Forward Dressing Station. On the way there, Black moaned and drank as much water as the orderly could give him. I lay back contentedly until I was suddenly tortured with the thought of Robin lying out with his smashed leg and his amorphous, whimpering companion. My determination to make amends and to go back to him had come to this.

You should have made Bert go back with you then: you knew the way, said the accusing voices of my thoughts. But I couldn't have gone back while Black was so bad and had no vehicle to take him back, said the defence. You never thought of Black, I reflected, as the ambulance halted.

The door was opened by a Medical Captain of the Brigade Field Ambulance, whom I knew. He was very cheerful, and gave us both morphia injections. To me – Black refusing it – he gave also a double tot of brandy, and I sank into a cheerful stupor, full of pleasant dreams until we reached the New Zealand Main Dressing Station, and were taken into a large square E.P.I.P. tent and laid out in rows on the sand floor. For perhaps five minutes I lay there. I think I had already acquired the little card which was placed on my chest like a mortuary label and went with me all the way to the Delta, stating my rank and name, and the fact that I had multiple mine wounds, comments on the nature and position of which were added by the various doctors who saw me en route. Anyway, if I had not yet got my little card, it was here I got it, for I was looking at it when the light from the door was shut out by more stretcher-bearers entering. I was immensely relieved to see that Robin, pale but conscious and interested in his surroundings, was their burden. I called out to him and he turned his head to see me and answered 'Hallo' with an expression of weariness and surprise. He was carried through into another tent. The M.D.S. was formed by numbers of tents joined to one another at different angles, like dominoes.

Presently I was carried through into another tent, and laid on the floor again. I lay here for perhaps an hour, wide awake with hunger, for I had had nothing to eat since the evening of the day before, except a little cold bacon and biscuits very early in the darkness before we moved off to attack the Wadi. There was a great deal to watch in this tent. Mine was one of four stretchers on the floor along one side of it. Opposite us were four stretchers placed on trestles. Above the occupants of these stretchers – I saw that one of them was Black – depended large inverted bottles from the nozzles of which red rubber tubes led to the wounded men's wrists, to which they were somehow attached. This at least was how it appeared to me, peering across the gloom of the tent. In some of these bottles was a colourless liquid and in others blood. Presently Robin was brought in, and after lying beside me, talking about something or other so quietly that I could hardly hear him, he was lifted up beside Black as soon as a place was vacant, and had one of the tubes fastened to him. Black's bottle was half full of colourless liquid. Robin's was a bottle of blood.

A canvas partition screened the other half of the tent from us, and occasionally surgeons in white overalls could be seen moving about as they crossed and recrossed a tear in the partition. There were orderlies moving about among us all, making people comfortable, supplying us impartially with urine bottles or tin mugs of soup. I chose soup.

There was a good deal of noise in the tent, too. The orderlies made jokes or shouted instructions across to each other, and stopped to ask the men on the stretchers questions, either medical or in the way of polite conversation. A man whose face was covered entirely in bandages, on a stretcher in the dim corner at the end of my line, kept sitting up and was calling at regular intervals, 'Jack. Eh. Jack.' At first I thought he was trying to attract an orderly's attention, and one of them did go across to him, but to his inquiry the bandaged man only answered: 'Jack. 'Ere, Jack. Take these,' while the orderly pushed him slowly down on to the stretcher, saying: 'Jack's not here.'

And as soon as the orderly had turned away from him he propped himself on his elbow, and said: 'Jack. 'Ere's Mr Simpson's binoculars.' He had been one of John's crew. Below the noise of this delirious talk and the voices of the orderlies, there was a moaning, so regular that it might have been made by some machinery inside the man who moaned, coming from the stretcher next to that of the delirious man. Cruikshank would have drawn this interior well, and Hogarth would have made a shot at it.

I was picked up again and taken into the operating theatre beyond the partition. Here a dark young man, a surgeon, said: 'I'm just going to clean up your wounds a bit.' I hauled myself off my stretcher on to the operating table. At my ear a voice said something like: 'A New Zealander is someone who wears braces, has false teeth, and calls his best friend a bastard,' and added: 'Do you agree?' I was not much surprised at this remark, so I suppose some other conversation which I've forgotten must have led up to it. But I could not at the moment find a tactful answer to the tall, rather bald New Zealand surgeon who had said it. Luckily he did not wait for my mumbled answer, but held up a hypodermic syringe, and said: 'I'm going to stick this in your arm. I want you to tell me when you feel sleepy.' He inserted the point of it deftly and painlessly, and pressed the plunger. After a second or two I felt a faint drowsiness and said: 'Now I'm beginning to feel sleepy.' 'Does it feel good?' said his voice, already disembodied; and I had just time to murmur, 'Not bad,' before I was unconscious.

I woke, it seemed, a moment later, to feel an excruciating pain in the wound in my left thigh, which I suppose they were scraping out. The pain restored all my faculties, and I shouted out, 'Stop. Hey! The anaesthetic's working off.' The pain stopped, and I sank through a mutter of voices into oblivion. Presently I was vaguely aware of being moved, and of being on my stretcher again, still in the theatre. I opened my eyes, and said to someone bending over me. 'How long was I out?' 'About seven minutes,' he said. 'How do you feel?' 'Like a most almighty hangover.' My head was aching as if it were being hit with a sledge. Whoever it was offered me some soup, but I felt so dizzy raising my head to sip, that I refused it, and was borne away into another tent, where I lay for some hours without moving. The blur of voices in the tent resolved itself into individual tones and at last became intelligible. I opened my eyes at a well-known tone and saw another face quite hidden in bandages. 'Is that Sergeant Bayley?' I said, and his cheerful voice assented. 'There's your driver here as well, sir. He's over there.' Other voices joined in. The whole row beside me were from the regiment, chiefly men from the Shermans; masks of bandage and gauze hid their faces, with holes from which the lashless eyes looked and huge swollen mouths protruded. Some

145

of them had been in the hole I had left. 'The Jerries came and leaguered in the area,' said one of them. 'They found us in the hole, and put a sentry over us. Then they blew the tanks up. They blew your Crusader up, sir, took the kit off it first. We went to sleep. When we woke up, the Jerries were gone: then Captain Pyeman come, and got us out on his dingo.' After more conversation, we slept.

Daylight woke me in the morning, and a tremendous hunger. Presently orderlies came with plates of rather unappetizing biscuit porridge – simply sodden lumps of biscuit in a paste of crumbs and water, with no noticeable addition of sugar and condensed milk. I ate this quickly, and drank a mug of tea. The burned men were managing to cram spoons somehow between their immense lips, holding the spoons in their hands covered with thick gloves of bandage. Presently an orderly came back with a tray of Bovril and some plates of whitish liquid in which indefinable pasty objects were floating and disintegrating. 'All you burn casualties,' said the orderly. 'You can't have solid diet. You're for liquid diet.' Seeing they had already empty plates in their hands from which they had painstakingly supped up the wet biscuit, he took these away and said: 'Well, you may as well have the liquid diet, anyway.' I was given a plate of the tasteless white liquid, but disliked it and was able to get a cup of Bovril instead.

Afterwards some people's wounds were dressed. My own dressings did not need renewing, and I lay watching in fascination while the dressings of a man beside me, who had burnt hands, were removed. When the dressings were off, the entire skin of his hand was peeled off in elastic rolls, which were cut away with scissors, while he watched without any appearance of suffering, or even of much interest, a cigarette drooping from his lip. Later in the morning I was put in the ambulance again, still unwashed, and began the next journey, to the Casualty Clearing Station. I seemed to have some recollection that there were sisters at C.C.S.s and hoped to be out of the hands of orderlies. Here I was put down in an identical tent, except that there were iron beds, which rose on either side of me as I lay on my stretcher.

146

A New Zealand Sister came in. She looked like a story-book nurse, clean, slim, pretty and smiling. She knew all the right things to say, and missed nobody. She came and looked at my card, and I looked up, incredibly filthy and bearded: glaring at her, I expect, as I do when I am embarrassed, in a ferocious way. She was an old campaigner, it seemed, and knew the order of things. She said: 'Would you like a meal?' A meal. Not just something to eat. A meal. And she brought me salmon and salad in a china plate, and a bowl of fruit salad and condensed milk. After that, it was clearly necessary I should be washed, and she came back and cut away the remains of my clothes. I said: 'May I keep the big pocket of my battledress trousers?' She cut it out and handed it to me as a bag to put the contents of my other pockets in. I found I had three pounds, my identity card, some letters, and a pair of spectacles; not a bad selection. I was washed, and given a pair of clean, grey flannel pyjamas to put on.

Before evening, we were moved on, a batch of us, to another C.C.S. It was a long journey, with an Indian driver. He drove that ambulance in a manner almost to persuade us that it had square wheels.

A man on the stretcher opposite moaned all the way, talking to himself, or to us, I don't know which. I was beginning to be accustomed to the regularity and monotony of wounded men's moaning. This man said: 'Oh. Oh. I didn't want to fight. Oh. I didn't want to fight. Oh. I didn't want to fight,' every four seconds, I judged, for ten lurching miles. Then he altered it suddenly to: 'Had a good job. Had a good job,' and, changing quickly again: 'Bags o' money. Bags o' money. Oh. Oh. Oh. Bags of money. Packets of money.' But in the end he came again to: 'I didn't want to fight,' and I think we were all glad when the ambulance arrived at the British C.C.S. At the gate a very efficient and sprucely dressed R.S.M. took our cards, transcribed the information on them, and the other ranks were taken out. The officers were trundled round and put in an officers' ward. Here we lay, getting hungry again. About six o'clock in the evening, a very old orderly, who walked with difficulty, brought us a plate of cold tinned vegetables, a thin slice of cheese, and a mug of tea. When we had eaten it another orderly, who seemed as decrepit as the first, came and removed the plate and mug. I had a terrible and quite abortive struggle with a bedpan shaped like a shovel, which left me quite exhausted, trembling with exertion and embarrassment, and determined on self-enforced constipation in future. Later in the evening the two decrepit orderlies brought tea. One of them stated in a quavering voice that we could have Oxo instead if we liked. I asked for Oxo and my mug of tea was taken away from me. Thinking of the brisk, spruce young orderlies I had seen in Base hospitals, I wondered why the R.A.M.C. found it necessary to post these poor old creatures, who should surely have stayed at home, to a busy desert C.C.S. quite near the front line. There was no sign of my Oxo. I called out: 'Orderly,' but neither of the old men came, although I could hear them pottering about behind the screen at the end of the tent. At length one of them came in on some business of his own, and I said: 'Am I getting my Oxo?' He looked at me like the old porter in the railway sketch, of whom the stationmaster says: 'You mustn't mind Robinson, sir, he's a bit hasty – like.' 'What was it you wanted, sir?' he asked. 'Oxo, please.' 'There's tea,' he said, unbelievably. 'But there's Oxo, too, isn't there?' He considered. 'Oh, yes,' he admitted. 'You can have Oxo, sir.' After two or three minutes he brought me a cup of tea. This really happened.

A bustling young sister, bulging absurdly in an issue battle-dress, came in to say good night to us. Lights were put out, and we slept until we were woken at five in the morning. It was cold. The orderlies brought us a cup of tea each, and eight huge red pills, like aniseed balls. We ate these with difficulty, and were carried out into the open air shivering. The Indian driver was waiting for us and jolted us, apparently across country, to a landing ground, where we arrived about six. A crew of Air Force ground staff were waiting to load us on to a plane. They were cursing with a great show of vocabulary at having to get up so early, and took no sort of care about getting the stretchers out, bumping and banging them without any apology. Although I was not in any pain, and could stand plenty of bumps, there were one or two badly wounded men who moaned and gasped with pain. I wished I could have the strength to get up and knock the orderlies about. They did not fix the stretchers properly in the slings, and two of them fell out as the plane taxied across the bumpy ground on to the tarmac. There were two orderlies of the R.A.M.C. with us, who managed to fix these stretchers. The actual flight was a rough one. The plane dipped and swayed until I could not stand it any longer, and lying helplessly, flat on my back, suddenly discharged a stream of tea ensanguined with the juice of the eight pills out of my mouth, like a whale spouting. One of the orderlies mopped me up in a perfunctory way, and the journey continued. After an hour or two we landed at El Adem – it was now about eleven o'clock in the morning. For half an hour we lay in the plane. Outside the window, I could see some R.A.F. men sitting on a packing case in the shadow of the wind and eating bread and cheese. Presently they also devoured packets of chocolate. I realized I was very hungry. Our orderly went off to see if he could find us some tea, and at last returned with about half a mug each from the R.A.F. cookhouse. We lay in the aircraft for five hours; apparently the C.C.S. which had sent us off had forgotten to notify the C.C.S. receiving us, and there were no ambulances waiting for us. They came at last, and we were removed to a more luxurious C.C.S., where we arrived in time for a very good evening meal, our first food of the day, with the exception of eight pills. We stayed four days in this, our last C.C.S., hearing occasionally the crash of German bombs on Tobruk, and waiting for a train to the Delta. At last we were driven to the station and packed into the bunks on the hospital train for the last three days of our journey to hospital.

During this time I had had many moments of misgiving, when it seemed I might be parked, first in hospital at Barce, and then at Tobruk. I was very relieved to find myself at last on a train which in three days' time would be standing in Alexandria station. These three days and nights were long ones. The train travelled slowly and stopped often altogether, at first, although it picked up speed on the last part of the journey. The medical staff, apart from a charming matron, a sergeant-major and an apparently competent M.O., all of whom paid only fleeting visits, were a scrawny assistant matron who wandered through the carriage as though she were looking for a lavatory; a buxom, ageing sister who was almost instantly known to us as the old grey mare; and one orderly, who lounged about with a cigarette drooping from his lip. The men in the bunks near me were an R.E. major who had been blown up on a mine in a fifteen-hundredweight; a young staff captain who had fallen off an armoured car, and dislocated his shoulder; a mysterious Semitic civilian, fully dressed, apparently a merchant sailor; a young lieutenant of the Rifle Brigade, wearing an M.C. ribbon, who had a poisoned foot, and an R.A.F. aircraftman who, hundreds of miles behind the front line, had gone out for a walk and tripped an S mine, exactly as I had done on the battlefield. The bunks were in three tiers a side.

The major, Jock someone or other, was a very pleasant chap, and made a good deal of amiable conversation. He said there was never time in a running battle to probe carefully for mines yard by yard, and the only thing to do was to drive along a road until you blew up. 'I got five miles before I went up,' he said. 'Think how long it would have taken to go along all that way with detectors. You chaps in tanks would have been cursing away, wondering why you were being kept hanging about.' His driver had been killed, having had both legs blown off. He himself had a fractured shin, and was most impatient at being sent so far back with it. He had been in France with 50 Division, and was one of the few original members of the Division left. He said he was afraid if he came so far back he would get posted before he could get back to them. It was the third time he had been blown up: he himself had laid many mines and had invented a mine of which he was very proud, and which had been generally adopted.

The staff captain, who could walk, did all he could to help everyone, and managed to find us books. Mine was *Dodo* and I spoke very little until I had read it through twice, quite lost and contented in that luxurious, indolent Edwardian world. There could be no kinder reading to tired minds and emotions. After that I began Nora Waln's book about her German holidays, which did not amuse or interest me nearly so much as her Chinese diary, *The House of Exile*. I wished I had that instead, and left reading for conversation. The merchant seaman, or whatever he was, spoke to no one, and none of us spoke to him, because we did not know what language to use. The M.O., when he came on his rounds, employed very slow and painstaking English, and received low, muttered replies which I could not interpret.

The aircraftman groaned a great deal, and we all called out for the orderly once, when he seemed in more than usual pain, and complained of being cold. The orderly did not come until Nigel, the staff captain, went to fetch him. He took no notice at first of the aircraftman, but busied himself about the unnecessary folding of some blankets on an empty bunk, saying in a stupid, angry voice: 'All right, all right, I'll see about you in a minute,' until I told him to bloody well drop the blankets and do something at once for the aircraftman, or I would report him to the M.O., and make bloody sure he got punished. At this he moved, muttering, across to the aircraftman's bunk, and bent over him. The ash fell off his cigarette on to the wounded man. Presently he rearranged the blankets clumsily, and the aircraftman cried out. The orderly went away down the corridor, and did not come back. Later the old grey mare came in. She seemed to have unlimited time for hanging about and chatting to the men who were fit enough to flirt with her (and tolerant enough of her slack body, rolling old eye and false teeth). I called her attention to the aircraftman, who was still clearly in great pain, and asked if he could be given a sedative, but she said he must wait till the M.O. made his evening round. The M.O. did come after the man had been in great pain for another hour, and immediately gave him morphia, and rearranged his pillows to support him where he had no wounds.

On the second morning, I woke with a fair amount of pain in the wound in the small of my back, and when the old grey mare made her appearance, I persuaded her to remove the bandage and have a look at it. She did this, but said the wound 'looked all right', and replaced the old dressing. The M.O. did not stop anywhere near me on his round, so I wasn't able to ask him about it. Later, when my dressings were taken off in hospital, a sister pulled out with her fingers a sliver of steel about a third of an inch long and an eighth in thickness.

20

Towards evening of the third day, the train pulled into a large station. There was no window on my side, and I asked where it was. 'Alexandria,' said the sergeant-major, who had been supervising the off-loading of some patients. 'Are we getting out here?' I asked, hopefully. 'No, sir. You're going on.' My spirits fell, until I reflected there was still a chance that Cairo was our destination. But I was asleep before we stopped in Cairo station – if we did stop there, and woke up in a grey half-light, with the draught blowing in from an open door. There was a good deal of bustling about on the pavement, a mixture of shouts in English and gabbling monotones in some native language. At last I was heaved out and tilted on my stretcher until two bearers on the cold space beside the line took me. They were South African native ambulance drivers, and thrust me into a dark ambulance, where I lay shivering for a few minutes. Then there were the noises of boots on metal, the clang of the cab door, grinding of an initial gear, and the engine revving as the ambulance moved. We were going at speed along a tarmac road, and after some quarter of an hour's driving, swung into a wide drive and halted in front of a dim building. My stretcher was lifted out on to a two-wheeled trolley, with handles, like a coster's barrow, and I was propelled through doors, into a long, lighted room, crowded with men on similar trollies, to whom girls in khaki overalls were giving sausage rolls, cakes and hot tea. One of them came and offered me a sausage roll and a cake. When she spoke, I realized they were all Palestinians. Presently an R.A.M.C. warrant officer came and said to me peremptorily: 'Where's you card?' After some fumbling, I found it under my blankets. He read it to himself, and then said, aloud, in a puzzled voice, 'L.T. What's that? Lieutenant?' He looked at me hard.

'Are you an officer?' he said in a tone of, 'Don't try that stuff with me.' 'Yes,' I said in apology. 'Well, I don't know. I thought you was an other rank. You've got other rank's pyjamas on,' he added, accusingly. I explained how I had come by them. The sergeant-major scratched himself. 'I suppose you want to go to the officers' ward,' he said. He called a tough-looking Jewess. 'Here,' he said, 'take this one to the officers' wards,' and I was wheeled out into the darkness again, looking back over my shoulder with a nostalgia for the sausage rolls.

A sister met us at the door of the officers' wards. 'Did you get left behind?' she said, as though I was a lost Pekinese, in a cajoling voice, and called: 'Antonio!' A little, black-jowled Italian sailor, blinking the sleep out of his eyes, came forward from the shadows of the passage. 'Take this officer to L.4.' I was wheeled away again, down a passage and suddenly swung sideways in at a doorway, and there were two beds, with Jock in one of them, who greeted me amiably. I got into the other bed, amazed at the feel of clean sheets and springs, and admiring books on a shelf, blue and white check curtains, and a strip of carpet. Jock was demanding food, and presently a cup of tea and some salmon sandwiches were brought us. I ate these, comparing them unfavourably with my lost sausage rolls. A bowl of hot water was swung across my lap on a bedside table for me to sit up and wash. Then I lay back to sleep. But it seemed I had hardly closed my eyes, before a Sudani boy, grinning a typical grin, stood before me, saying amiably: 'Eggs. Beckun. Tamam. Quois awi,' with a loaded tray, two fried eggs, bacon, fried bread, coffee, bread and butter and marmalade. I cannot describe the glow which came over me at this wonderful apparition, with all its comfortable implications. After this third, and most successful, breakfast I dozed again, deciding lazily what I would do. I would write fourteen letters at least, to everyone of my acquaintance in the Middle East. I would need some clothes for when I got up. The last C.C.S., where I had been washed and shaved, had presented me with a towel, and a sponge bag containing soap, facecloth, blades, and a razor, though I had still to buy a brush. I could write to David in Cairo, to buy me an N.Z. battledress, and to Titsa, and Milena, and Renée, and Olga, and Mary, and that girl in Rechowoth – Hasida, or whatever her name was. I must send a cable to Mother, and then write her a letter with a diagram of where the wounds were. Then I must write to Edward and Tom, in that strange world which was suddenly so remote. Presently I slept again.

ZEM ZEM

WE had sat opposite the mountain, crowned with its Arab village, for about two weeks, when the campaign ended. The village had become known as Nottingham Castle, because of its resemblance to the trade-mark on Players' cigarette packets. I arrived from convalescence to Egypt by air, a day or two after the regiment had come out of action and had taken up these positions. The tanks, spaced out in packets of two, with fifty or one hundred yards between packets, were on a broad, flat plain, covered with long grass and occasional flowers. Half right of our front lay the skeletons of trees and houses; all that remained of Enfidaville, which was still under enemy shell-fire. Seen from this distance – some three or four miles – it still looked as though a town was there. Transport moved up and down across our front on the Enfidaville–Kairouan road. And beyond, between the road and the mountain, where we had artillery positioned in the fig and peach orchards, there was a continuous haze from the smoke of enemy shell-bursts. Sometimes a big Italian shell, coming over the mountain, would hit the crest, and a plume of smoke hang over Nottingham Castle. Smoke could be still in the air for fifteen or twenty minutes, gradually disintegrating into the heat-haze. The days were hot and still, the sky often an unrelieved blue.

I had come up in the aircraft carrying mails and newspapers to Sfax, with six or seven other officers. There were so many of us in this Hudson that we had to crowd to one end to get the tail off the ground. We left Shepheards Hotel at seven in the morning, landed and lunched in an R.A.F. Sergeants' Mess, at the old German landing ground at Marble Arch, and had arrived at Sfax aerodrome by half past four. During the last hour of our flight, coming inland from flying high over the minute wrinkles of the Mediterranean Sea, the deep sea blue gave way, not to brown or yellow desert country, but to an almost European

155

pattern of towns and cultivation. From Sfax transit camp, we went up to the Left Out of Battle Camp near El Djem, where there is a huge, surprising Roman amphitheatre at the turn of the road.

At this camp a lorry from the regiment collected me. I didn't arrive with any enthusiasm for battle, but rather in a mood of dullness or apathy. From my news, letters from Edward, and rumours and accounts at the R.A.C. base depot in Cairo, it seemed as though the regiment could never recover from the punishment it had taken. On the first morning of my sick leave in Palestine, sitting at breakfast among the pavement tables of a Tel Aviv café, I bought a paper, and read of Piccadilly Jim's death.

It was impossible to realize it. The whole moment and everything in it – the coloured tables, the sunglare on the pavements, the white houses and the morning pedestrians – seemed suddenly part of a dream. Piccadilly Jim, with all his faults of occasionally slapdash and arbitrary conduct, had been a brave man and a colonel of whom we could be proud. Of whom, I discovered, somewhat to my own surprise, I had been proud myself. He was an institution: it seemed impossible that in a moment a metal splinter had destroyed him. He had embodied in himself all the regimental characteristics he had been at pains to create. That assumption of superiority, that dandyism, individuality, and disregard of the duller military conventions and regulations, had made the regiment sometimes unpopular – the Australians could not understand men who polished their badges for a battle – but always discussed and admired. We knew we were better than anyone else, and cared for no one. But the focal point of this confidence was Piccadilly Jim. I was amazed to find, reading of his death, that I felt like a member of the old régime who looks on at a bloody revolution.

But that was not all. Piccadilly Jim, killed as one might say, typically, while he was standing up in his tank, shaving under shell-fire, had already been translated into a full Colonelcy at Brigade, handing over the regiment to Guy. When I arrived at Base depot I found a letter from Edward which wrung my heart, it was so utterly dejected. Tom had been killed by a shell: another institution gone, and someone on whom I now saw that I (as I had remarked of everyone else) had come to rely, 'as a sort of Universal Aunt.' All his success in the regiment, all his plans for great deals and the making of horses, and equestrian honours for his two little daughters, wiped away by one shell-burst: as if by one devastating, cynical comment of God, *l'éternel voleur des énergies*. And at the L.O.B. camp, a trooper who had just come from the regiment told me Guy had been killed by a shell as he was making a forward recce in his jeep along the road on the enemy side of Enfidaville. 'The finest colonel we ever had,' this man said. 'He only had the regiment a week or two, but he done bloody well.' And so a shell had got Guy too, the last of our traditional heroes.

All the emphasis was on shells. Mick, the Navigating Officer, said to me as soon as he saw me: 'Hullo. How are you? You went back at Zem Zem, didn't you? Good Lord, you don't know what it's like, then. This shell-fire now is – well ... it's bloody awful, it's like nothing you ever saw in your life.' The new colonel had arrived, a scarred young cavalryman, wearing the ribbons of the Order of St. John of Jerusalem and the Military Cross. I found the regiment at an hour's notice.

I had brought up with me an infantry officer, a boy from the Black Cats, 56 Division, coming straight from the Ski School in the Lebanon to join his unit in action for the first time. He was nervous, and afraid he might disgrace himself in his first battle; we did all we could to make him feel more comfortable, and to persuade him that he would probably neither disgrace nor dis-tinguish himself, but simply enter the battle and emerge again, having done his job. He went away next morning to join his unit, and went into the attack with 56 Division, which we were to follow up and support.

But this attack did not go according to plan, and the Black Cats were driven back off their objective with such heavy casualties that the tank attack was called off, and the regiment was not in action again during the last days of the campaign. We stayed in our positions, like a terrier at a rat-hole. The

157

officer who had spent the night with us survived, and I met him again a week or two later, full of the same elation – a true feeling of gladness to be alive – as I had felt after the battle of Alamein.

Meanwhile, the attack being called off, I was sent away in a three-ton lorry to look for wine and sheep. There was a rumour of wine at Gafsa: and as a more military reason for travelling, I was told to get hold of some jeep spares. We drove all day through battered Sousse and Sfax, and down the coast road, nearly to Gabes. The green country lasted almost all the way, the road-side littered, though not so thickly as of old, with the derelict trucks, tanks and guns of both sides. There were the occasional carcasses of planes.

We ran through a belt of desert inland from Gabes and up through the dry, brown hills to Gafsa. At Gafsa's outskirts we suddenly crossed a stream, fringed with fresh grass and coolly reflecting overhanging palms. Here the Americans had put up two huge notices:

THE FIRST ARMY WELCOMES THE EIGHTH ARMY

and

2 CORPS – GONE TO GABES

We ran through some buildings, and drew up beside an American Negro sentry. Whether this man had ever had a job as a comic Negro on the stage, or whether Negroes do always speak like that, I haven't enough experience to say. But it is beyond doubt that, when we asked him the name of the town, he scratched himself, and answered, after a tremendous pause: 'Well, I *did* know, but I done forgotten.' This reply delighted me.

After a few minutes we climbed into the town proper, and were directed to the wine control bureau, presided over by an unshaven but courteous French sergeant, who announced that we could have a litre of wine for each man, if we had a *bidon* in which to put it. There was a little tasting of wine, and in the spirit of comradeship thus induced, the Frenchmen invited us to lunch, and we contributed our tinned meat and vegetables and salmon to their cold meat, salad, potatoes, and various strongly flavoured vegetables.

Wines, not for sale, were produced, the meal culminating in the abrupt, zigzag departure of one of my drivers, who was assisted into the lorry, and went to sleep on my bedding, after first being sick on it. In his absence, toasts were drunk in brandy, and I took the photographs of the company, and, separately, the photograph of the miscreant, now dead to the world.

With some misgiving, I drove the truck out of Gafsa, steering between buildings like the Symplegades, those clashing rocks which rushed together upon the unwary ship which ventured between them. I had undertaken to transport a young man, a native of Sousse, home to his parents. He was dark and thin, with huge eyes, and armed with an imposing array of C.M.P. permits. Later we picked up another youth and two Free French soldiers of the Giraud variety (North African French, as opposed to the De Gaullists who had fought their way up with us; and the distinction was as sharp as that between the Eighth and First Armies). We drew some rations from the dump at a Forward Maintenance Centre, near Gabes, and spent the night out. The second young man was not very pleasant nor polite, and when I asked him if he had any bedding, replied: 'J'ai un lit – de vous,' and laughed heartily at his own wit, in contrast to his fellow-civilian, who said only: 'J'ai un burnous,' and was for sleeping in the sand until I persuaded him to sleep along the cushioned seat in the driver's cab, since he was the only one short enough for it.

We arrived in Sousse late next day, with Edouard – the young man with dark eyes – and two sheep as passengers. The sheep we had forcibly taken from an Arab shepherd for 600 francs the two, or 30s. each. This was the method suggested by the shepherd who was not allowed to sell them of his own free will. It was fairly clear that the owners would never see the 600 francs. Edouard took us in to see his family. The house was in perfect order, having been used as a German Officers' Mess. His mother bustled about all over the place, full of an embarrassing gratitude, referring to us constantly as 'les pauvres' because we were going back towards the battle, and laying before us a beautifully prepared dinner, with wine and vermouth, iced. There were two small children, a boy and a girl, both without any shyness and full of life: and a daughter about sixteen, as shy and clumsy as her young brother and sister were unaffected and spry. Edouard's father, a medical man and amateur painter of nudes, allegorical or classical illustrations, and landscapes, of which the house was full, lamented that the Germans – who had otherwise behaved 'very correctly' – had taken his Wattman paper and Windsor & Newton paints.

His pictures were technically good, but lacking, except for some of the small landscapes, in any emotion of true feeling – in style a little following Puvis de Chavannes. He had been a corporal of Zouaves in the last war, and produced a box full of imposing medals: he and his fellow Zouaves had had a great success against the Germans, he said, 'Avec la baïonnette'. He pranced round the room to demonstrate.

After dinner, we listened to the wireless and talked. Edouard, though young, was, it appeared, one of the foremost poets of Tunisia, and had received a medal from the Tunisian Literary Academy – Société des Amis de la Littérature Française de Tunisie, or whatever it was called. I was shown his poems, which were all very similar, very mannered, musical, and innocently sensual, and immediately echoed in my ear:

> *les sanglots longs*
> *des violons*
> *de l'automne*
> *blessent mon coeur*
> *d'une langueur*
> *monotone.*

That night, I slept, after a welcome shower, in a real bed, with clean, lavender-scented sheets of pale blue linen. My two drivers, one with a well-merited hangover, slept in the back of the truck with the sheep, of which one broke its bonds during the night, and very nearly escaped. Before they went out to the truck, they also had showers – leaving a tremendous deposit in the bathroom which I managed to clear up before Madame should see it.

After coffee and rolls in the morning, we returned to the regiment, and delivered our freight, the sheep and some peaches bought in Sfax making up for the lack of wine. There was still no word of our going into action, and I was immediately sent off, with a mechanist sergeant and a driver, in a fifteen-hundred-weight to follow up a very strong rumour of jeep spares in 1st Army's area, and of whisky at a 1st Army N.A.A.F.I. at some monosyllabic place whose name I forgot. Also, said someone else, there is wine at Pichon. We drove all day, climbing through the hills on rough going and alarming spiral gradients. We went through Pichon, deciding to leave its investigation until our return journey, and arrived an hour or two before nightfall in a village perched on the hillside.

The name of this village also escapes me: it was among tall evergreens, and rainclouds seemed to rush together over it as we entered the single street. Torrents of water descended the hill with us, and the truck, which I was driving, began to turn round and slither sideways, more like a piece of furniture than a car. I managed to skid off the road into the shelter of some trees, and halted an inch or two from the back of an old black Citroen, which was standing with a mass of such vehicles under the trees. A French officer came up to me, and asked what I wanted. 'Only to avoid the rain,' I said, but he would not accept this small aim. He invited us to dinner – my sergeant and driver with his men, and myself with the officers. My chaps agreed to this, and I said good night to them and staggered away up the hill behind the adjutant – for it was the adjutant who had met us – to the officers' mess.

In a large tent, among a litter of beds, chairs and equipment, I was introduced to three lieutenants, two young, one of whom wore American clothes which he said he had bought for two bottles of ration wine – and one bucolic middle-aged person, who later admitted to being a farmer by profession. The Commanding Officer of this detachment, a Captain, with grey hair, healthily red skin and light, twinkling eyes, arrived later. Dinner would be ready in half an hour, and we made desultory conversation. After a quarter of an hour, we heard a motor cycle turn off the road, and come towards the tent. A tall, thin, unshaven lieutenant was riding on it. 'They have taken Tunis and Bizerta,' he said. I did not believe him.

Nor, at first, did the others. But he gave the sources of his information, which were official, and reliable enough. They explained that all of them were Tunisian French, and that the Captain had his wife and children in Tunis. I must understand that it was a great day for them, and for the Captain in particular. We sat down at a table laid in the back of a huge Italian covered lorry, to a meal of fresh mutton, vegetables, macaroni, and bread, butter, and cheese, washed down with a much better red wine than any I had yet tasted in Tunisia. After a pint or two of wine, the fluency of my French, and my ability to follow the conversation, were surprising. Toasts were drunk amid a good deal of badinage, in brandy. I asked if the men had the same food, and was told, 'yes'. Was it a fact, they asked, that in the British army we ate things out of tins? We adjourned to the tent. 'Le Lieutenant,' said the bucolic man, confidently, indicating the youngest of them, 'va se saouler. Il est déjà un peu gris.' In the tent three bottles of Canadian whisky were waiting.

Our tumblers were filled about two-thirds full of neat whisky, and the Captain, twinkling more than ever, announced a toast with a slightly theatrical gesture: 'A la Victoire.' Glasses were tilted amidst declamations. Each man held his glass out, empty. To empty mine had not been easy: but every glass was at once refilled, as full as ever, and the Captain cried: 'A notre cher, vieux camarade d'la Huitième Armée.' I, not to be outdone, replied with great conviviality with a toast to my hosts. Glasses were again recharged. Another toast. Among the glasses held out, mine alone was full. 'A bas la Huitième Armée, n'a pas d'courage,' exclaimed the Captain, with volume, but little clarity. The youngest lieutenant slumped to the floor, where he vomited miserably. 'Ah!' shouted the company. 'Le lieutenant, il est fini. Dehors, mets le dehors,' and the body was removed. Presently the bringer of good news sat down on one of the beds, head in hands. But the others continued to wave their glasses about, drinking toast after toast. In this way I succeeded in pouring my last two glasses of whisky on the floor, though with reluctance. I had remembered the necessity for an early start in the morning.

The Captain, in the act of announcing another toast, fell backwards into a corner, where he lay, still crying his toast amiably, his eyes twinkling like harbour lights. I decided to go out and make myself sick, so as to be fit for work in the morning. The bucolic lieutenant and the one in American clothes, who had remained sober, tried to dissuade me, but I knew it was necessary, and excusing myself, went out. When I came back, they had laid out a palliasse for me, and I lay down and drifted into an uncomfortable stupor. I woke in the morning with them all snoring around me.

I sat up and looked about. My head whirled for a moment, and then settled to a steady, thumping ache. The Captain had been lifted up and put in bed. Presently the unshaven lieutenant, blacker-jawed than ever, sat up, clutched his head, and sank back. The farmer awoke next, and asked me how I felt. I sat up on my palliasse again, at the foot of the Captain's high bed, from which a voice, as though from another world, said: 'Où est la Huitème Armée?' I spoke up, but this only provoked a muttering of: 'N'ont pas de courage. Savent pas boire, ces polissons d'la Huitième.' 'Au contraire,' said the farmer, in my defence. 'Le Lieutenant a beaucoup bu. Il était le seul qui restait debout,' and added: 'Le Lieutenant est gentleman. Il est allé dehors pour dégueuler.'

An orderly arrived with some welcome black coffee, and I went out and threw a bucket of water over my head. Presently the Captain, groaning, was assisted out, and had the same done for him. I dressed, and went to find my sergeant and driver. They, too, had had a merry evening, but looked fitter than I felt. We started out half an hour later, leaving the Captain in bed, again complaining, probably with some reason, of his headache.

We halted, overlooking a wide valley, to shave and breakfast, and moved on to our first destination, the N.A.A.F.I., where

we spent about £40 of regimental money, and filled the truck
with whisky, beer, cordial, and cigarettes. Then we struck out
towards Beja, enquiring everywhere for an American Ordnance
depot. Beja, shell-torn as all Tunisian towns, could sell us nothing, and held no ordnance depot. At last we found one, where an
American officer paid me £5 for my Italian Biretta automatic,
throwing in two hundred Camels and half a dozen tubes of
Barbasol as a bonus. He was delighted with his purchase, and
kept clicking it as though it were a cap pistol, saying to himself:
'Sure is a mean little gun.' But he had no jeep spares. We
eventually got a few front springs and a coil, and had to be content with that.

We spent the night at a farmhouse, and struck up towards
Medjez-el-Bab, to see if we could get to Bone, where wine and
jeeps were said to abound. Near Medjez, we passed a P.O.W.
cage, filled to overflowing, and a little further up the road, on
which the drivers of dark green First Army vehicles regarded
our sandpaint with astonishment and interest, we saw a sign:

YOU ARE BEING TIMED.
DO NOT EXCEED YOUR SPEED LIMIT.

This in a battle area. 'No wonder they've taken such a muckin'
long time,' said my driver.

It did not seem likely that we should have time to reach
Bone, and the more I thought of the news, the more possible it
seemed that the regiment would advance. So we turned for
home. Night overtook us at Pichon, and we stayed with some
civilians, a gendarme and his wife, a married woman and her
two children, and a girl about nineteen years old. The gendarme
was in a good mood. During the German occupation he had been
beaten up by some Arabs, and Arabs had smashed the doors
and windows of the house we were now living in, and had
stolen or broken most of the furniture. Today he had arrested the
Arabs who had beaten him up. Some American soldiers came in
and had coffee with the family after supper. One of them spoke
Italian with the gendarme's wife, and played a guitar. The
Americans and my crew drank a bottle of the whisky, which I

still could not find any desire to drink, and which the French tasted and rejected with comical grimaces. In the morning I photographed our hostesses – the gendarme being gone early to work. We left Pichon for Kairouan, wondering if we should find the regiment gone, and the battle over.

But the shells were still falling between the mountain and the road, and the regiment still in its old positions. This time we were enthusiastically welcomed, although fourteen bottles of beer had been broken on our way back. A hen, for which the driver had swopped an old pair of khaki drill shorts, had laid two eggs without shells during the terrifying passage over the hill roads.

There was a variety concert given by the motor battalion attached to our brigade, on an open air stage, with a good many topical sketches and songs. During the performance a man in a German people's car and dressed in German uniform, with several iron crosses, arrived, gave a Nazi salute to actors and audience, and announced with a Teutonic intonation, that he came from 90 Light Division. 'Sit down, old boy, you're welcome. You've been with us a long time, now,' said someone on the stage. The man sat down, removing his false moustache, and bowing to the applause. 90 Light Division had fought us all the way from Alamein, and were still entrenched behind Enfidaville, the last German unit left in action.

That evening we had a cocktail party, for which all our captured tents were pieced together, an orchestra, consisting of a saxophonist, the trumpet-major playing an American jazz trumpet recaptured from the enemy, and a subaltern playing on an improvised set of drums, performed in the dusk outside, and curious cocktails were made with gin, red wine, and whisky, with occasional additions of lime cordial, and even condensed milk. The party was a great success.

The next morning, we heard that Von Arnim had been captured, and that Messe, the Italian General, had surrendered to General Freyburg. In the afternoon, coming back in a three-tonner from a bathing party at Hergla, we met a convoy of vehicles, stretching away up the road as far as we could see.

They were enemy vehicles of every size, crowded with Germans
or Italians, and with their own drivers, ten or fifteen without any
guard, and then perhaps someone in a jeep or on a motor-cycle;
driving themselves down the road to the P.O.W. cage at Hergla.
The drivers hooted for Eighth Army pedestrians to get out of
their way, and passed other slow-moving vehicles or signalled
people in a hurry to pass, with the utmost unconcern. The
Italians waved and shouted, and were in high spirits. The
Germans simply looked at us, or in front of them, without
expression. We watched the defeated army pass for perhaps a
quarter of an hour, before we could even find a gap through
which to turn across the main road and down on to the track
leading to the regiment.

That evening, we the remaining officers of 'A' Squadron, sat
over our whisky around the fifteen-hundredweight truck which
had come all the way from Alamein as the squadron office. From
a lighted tent came songs and laughter where our ten new
subalterns, who had joined as reinforcements during the last
few weeks, were carousing on gin and whisky and red wine.

Further away still, someone who had found a box of Verey lights was firing them off, three or four different colours, one after another into the deep blue night sky. But the distant booms and thuds which had been a background to all this for so long, were gone. We repeated over and over again in our thoughts and conversation that the battle was over. The continual halting and moving, the departure at first light, the shell-fire, the interminable wireless conversations – and the strain, the uncertainty of tomorrow, the fear of death: it was all over. We had made it. We stood here on the safe side of it, like swimmers. And Guy, lying under the flowers in Enfidaville cemetery, Piccadilly Jim, buried miles behind us, Tom, and all the others, back to the first casualties, during Rommel's attempt to break through to Alexandria; they didn't make it, but it's over for them, too.

And tomorrow, we said, we'll get into every vehicle we can find, and go out over the whole ground we beat them on, and bring in more loot than we've ever seen.

CPSIA information can be obtained at www.ICGtesting.com
Printed in the USA
BVOW02s1827201215

430692BV00001B/163/P